On Your Mark

READING FLUENCY PRACTICE AND ASSESSMENT

GRADE 6

HAMPTON-BROWN

Hampton-Brown
P.O. Box 223220
Carmel, California 93922
800-333-3510
www.hampton-brown.com

Printed in the United States of America

ISBN 0-7362-2479-3

Contents

Introduction

Benchmark Passages

Progress Monitoring Passages

Overview

What Is Reading Fluency?

Reading fluency is the ease, or naturalness, of reading. You can subjectively measure it by assessing **phrasing**, **syntax**, and **expressiveness**. That is, you can listen to a student read aloud and hear whether she or he is struggling to read word-by-word or is reading in a more natural, easy way.

But important questions remain.

- How can you know where the student is in relation to other students in that grade level and to grade-level norms?
- How can you know whether the student is improving over time?

The answer is straightforward: you can *objectively* measure the **accuracy** and **rate** that the student reads aloud. More than twenty-five years of research[1] has shown that listening to a child read aloud a grade-level-appropriate passage for one minute and calculating the number of words read correctly per minute provides a valid and highly reliable measure of reading fluency.

Reading fluency is strongly correlated to reading comprehension and, therefore, provides an efficient as well as valid procedure for:

- **identifying students who need a reading intervention program**. Research has shown that, in general, students whose fluency scores are in the 50th percentile have good reading comprehension of grade-level texts. Students whose scores fall in the 25th percentile or below fall in the at-risk range.
- **frequent progress monitoring**.
- **summative evaluation** of achievement.

The keys to producing reliable results from reading fluency assessments are:

- ensuring that the teacher follows the same, simple administration procedure with each student for each assessment, and
- having students read graded and equivalent passages that are written to represent a general, grade-level curriculum.

The only variable, then, is the student's performance, not the difficulty of the passage or the subjectivity of the administrator.

---

[1]**Selected References:**

Fuchs, L. S., Fuchs, D., & Maxwell, L. (1988). The validity of informal reading comprehension measures. *Remedial and Special Education*, 9(2), 20–28.

Shinn, M. R., Good, R. H., Knutson, N., Tilly, W. D., & Collins, V. (1992). Curriculum-Based Measurement of oral reading fluency: A confirmatory analysis of its relation to reading. *School Psychology Review*, 21(3), 459–479.

Reading Fluency Assessment Tools

On Your Mark provides graded and equivalent passages, as well as a simple administration procedure, to allow you to objectively measure and monitor students' reading fluency abilities over time.

The passages included in *On Your Mark* were carefully developed and tested with students by Kathryn B. Howe, Ph.D., and Michelle M. Shinn, Ph.D., to ensure that the passages within each grade level are similar in difficulty. The passages vary in length but all use the same font style and do not include pictures. This simple format helps students focus on reading. The passages are also "curriculum independent," which allows teachers to make decisions regardless of the instructional materials or program philosophy that is in place.

Tool	Purpose
Benchmark Assessment Passages: 3 graded and equivalent passages *See pages 18–23.*	• To screen students and identify those in need of reading intervention • To formally assess student reading fluency
Grade-Level Progress Monitoring Passages: 30 passages *See pages 26–85.*	• To frequently monitor student progress
Benchmark Improvement Report *See page 24.*	• To make programmatic decisions at the beginning of the year and report summative achievement
Progress Monitoring Report *See page 86.*	• To make student goals and progress visible • To provide timely data that can be used to inform instruction
AIMSweb™ (Achievement and Improvement Monitoring System): online reporting system from Edformation *Visit www.aimsweb.com/OnYourMark to learn more and to subscribe.*	• To allow students, families, teachers, and administrators to efficiently and effectively monitor student achievement

The Fluency Assessment Process

❶ Establish Benchmarks

Administer the three benchmark passages, three times per year:

- fall (beginning of the school year) for identification and program placement
- winter (middle of the school year)
- spring (end of the school year) for summative evaluation

In each administration, the median score is reported and compared to grade-level norms. Benchmark Assessments can be used for initial identification, for benchmarking against grade-level norms, and for summative evaluation of reading achievement at year's end.

Because several months elapse between each administration, there is no "practice effect" for students. Using the same yardstick during the year helps ensure accuracy in measuring changes in students' reading fluency over time.

❷ Set Goals

Compare the student's median score for the initial administration to the grade-level norms. The chart below shows percentiles and the number of words read correctly per minute for a large, national sample of sixth-grade students.

Grade 6 Reading Growth Table

Fall			Winter			Spring			
Number of Students	Percentile	Words Read Correctly	Number of Students	Percentile	Words Read Correctly	Number of Students	Percentile	Words Read Correctly	ROI
	90	181		90	198		90	211	0.8
	75	158		75	170		75	183	0.7
15,236	50	131	15,584	50	144	16,954	50	155	0.7
	25	101		25	113		25	125	0.7
	10	70		10	83		10	94	0.7

The last column on the right shows the Rate of Improvement (ROI) you might realistically expect for students to achieve. ROI is the end of year score minus the beginning of year score, divided by 36 weeks (or the mid-year score minus the beginning of year score divided by 18 weeks).

You can expect a student reading at a second-grade level to gain 0.7 to 1.2 words per week; however, you can expect a gain of only 0.7 to 0.8 words per week from a student functioning at a sixth-grade level. Set a realistic goal so that it is achievable for the student.

❸ Monitor and Report Progress

Fluency measures can be used for much more than initial placement into a reading program. They are also excellent tools to monitor students' progress over time and to inform daily classroom instruction. They are especially useful in both monitoring and motivating struggling readers.

- Fluency rates are more sensitive to gains than other reading tests. That is, it's easier to observe reading improvement. Students who set and achieve realistic goals become and stay motivated.
- Any adult—teachers, paraprofessionals, or parent volunteers—can administer fluency assessments with only brief training.
- The tests take only a few minutes per student to administer.

❹ Make Instructional Decisions

After determining a student's median score, use the normative performance chart to determine how each student compares to other students in the same grade nationally. The results are educational averages compiled using standard benchmark passages during the school year. Students scoring below the 50th percentile may benefit from additional instruction.

If the student's gains are higher than expected, raise the goal. If the student's scores decrease or remain the same for six successive weeks, consider an instructional intervention.

Administering the Tests

Because the assessment process is a standardized one, always administer the passages the same way each time you test a student.

Before Testing

Gather the following materials:
- a copy of the student version of the passage(s)
- a copy of the teacher version of the passage(s)
- a pen or pencil to mark the teacher version
- an accurate timer or stopwatch.

There are two versions of each benchmark and progress-monitoring passage: a student version and a teacher version. (See page 9.) The passages are identical except the teacher version includes word counts at the end of each line, name and date lines, and a scoring box. These features allow teachers to score tests and record results quickly for each student.

Choose a reasonably quiet area, away from distractions, where you can conduct the one-on-one assessment. The setting is important to ensure accurate test results.

Do not teach the passage in advance or allow students to practice reading the passages.

During Testing

Sit directly across from the student.

Place the student version of the passage in front of the student.

Place the teacher version in front of you, but shield it from students so that they cannot see what is marked. (A clipboard that can rest on your lap is effective.)

Keep the timer or stopwatch out of sight to keep students from focusing on speed.

Before starting, explain to students that
- you want them to read as well as they can, not as fast as they can.
- they should skip a word if they can't read it after three seconds.

If any student reads fewer than 10 words correctly in one minute, discontinue testing. You may wish to use passages from a lower grade level with such a student.

Mark a slash (/) through errors. Do not try to record everything a student says or does, and do not correct any errors during the test. The student should be the only one speaking during the test.

After one minute, mark a bracket after the last word read. Wait to tell the student to stop until they finish the sentence.

Grade 6 Progress Monitoring Passage #6

Student Version

Crystal's next door neighbor was a very large and strange man. He was well over six feet tall with feet the size of tennis rackets. Sometimes while riding the bus to school, Crystal saw him at the dump digging through piles of garbage. Sometimes while riding the bus home from school, she saw him walking down the sidewalk lugging a heavy burlap sack over his shoulder. Crystal never knew what was in the sack. She could only guess as she watched him open his front door and close it behind him. Her older brother, Jason, had an idea.

"Maybe the guy next door is so poor," he told Crystal one afternoon, "he has to go to the dump to scavenge for food. I bet he collects old boots and makes boot-leather soup." Crystal wrinkled her nose. She didn't like the sound of that.

"Do you think I should bring him some food?" she asked. "I could bring him some of the leftover cinnamon rolls Mom made last weekend." Jason was too busy laughing to answer. Crystal ignored her big brother. She knew he could be rude and mean sometimes.

The next morning before school, Crystal walked across the yard and knocked on her neighbor's front door. She knocked several times, but no one answered. Crystal left the tray of cinnamon rolls covered with tinfoil on his steps and ran to catch the bus. She didn't see the curtains twitch as she turned to leave, but she did see piles of rusty old pipes stacked in the backyard.

All day as Crystal sat in class, she wondered what her neighbor used those pipes for. When she got home, she found a clean plate and a folded piece of tinfoil on her front steps. She ran across her yard to her neighbor's door.

Before she could knock, the door opened. Her neighbor stood in the doorway towering over her. Crystal would have been scared to death had there not been a kind smile on his face and a sincere look in his eyes. He didn't say a word. Instead he handed her a beautiful set of silver wind chimes.

"How lovely," she said. "Thank you very much." Crystal now understood what her neighbor did with his burlap sack and his backyard full of pipes.

STUDENT COPY: Progress Monitoring Passage #6   30

© Edformation, Inc.

Teacher Version

Name _____ Date _____

Crystal's next door neighbor was a very large and strange man. He was well | 14
over six feet tall with feet the size of tennis rackets. Sometimes while riding the bus | 30
to school, Crystal saw him at the dump digging through piles of garbage. | 43
Sometimes while riding the bus home from school, she saw him walking down the | 57
sidewalk lugging a heavy burlap sack over his shoulder. Crystal never knew what | 70
was in the sack. She could only guess as she watched him open his front door and | 87
close it behind him. Her older brother, Jason, had an idea. | 98

"Maybe the guy next door is so poor," he told Crystal one afternoon, "he has to | 114
go to the dump to scavenge for food. I bet he collects old boots and makes boot- | 131
leather soup." Crystal wrinkled her nose. She didn't like the sound of that. | 144

"Do you think I should bring him some food?" she asked. "I could bring him | 159
some of the leftover cinnamon rolls Mom made last weekend." Jason was too busy | 173
laughing to answer. Crystal ignored her big brother. She knew he could be rude | 187
and mean sometimes. | 190

The next morning before school, Crystal walked across the yard and knocked on | 203
her neighbor's front door. She knocked several times, but no one answered. Crystal | 216
left the tray of cinnamon rolls covered with tinfoil on his steps and ran to catch the | 233
bus. She didn't see the curtains twitch as she turned to leave, but she did see piles | 250
of rusty old pipes stacked in the backyard. | 258

All day as Crystal sat in class, she wondered what her neighbor used those pipes | 273
for. When she got home, she found a clean plate and a folded piece of tinfoil on her | 291
front steps. She ran across her yard to her neighbor's door. | 302

Before she could knock, the door opened. Her neighbor stood in the doorway | 315
towering over her. Crystal would have been scared to death had there not been a | 330
kind smile on his face and a sincere look in his eyes. He didn't say a word. Instead | 348
he handed her a beautiful set of silver wind chimes. | 358

"How lovely," she said. "Thank you very much." Crystal now understood what | 370
her neighbor did with his burlap sack and his backyard full of pipes. | 383

| SCORE | words attempted in one minute | − | number of errors | = | words correct per minute (wcpm) |

© Edformation, Inc.

Grade 6 | TEACHER COPY: Progress Monitoring Passage #6   31

Scoring the Tests

The Basics of Scoring

On the teacher version of each passage, there are two features to help you score:

1. Numbers to the right of each line show the cumulative number of words.

2. Scoring boxes at the bottom help you calculate final scores.

   - Count the number of words attempted.

   - Subtract the number of errors from the number of words attempted.

   - This yields the number of words read correctly per minute (wcpm), as well as the number of errors, which is also useful to track.

Determine the Final Score

To determine the final score, first record the total number of words read. Then subtract the number of errors. For example, if Don read 141 words and made 3 errors, his wcpm is 138.

Use the median score of the three benchmark passages as the student's final score, and compare it to the grade level norms for the appropriate time of year. (See page 6.)

Definitions

Words Read Correctly (wcpm)
- A word pronounced correctly within context
- Self-corrections within three seconds

Errors
- Mispronunciations
- Substitutions
- Omissions
- Three-second pauses where the teacher tells the student to skip the word

Do Not Count as Errors
- Mispronunciations due to dialect or speech problems
- Repetitions
- Insertions

MARKING THE PASSAGE

Slashes indicate words that the student skips, omits, or mispronounces.

Name Don López   Date Sept. 6

One of the reasons Becky loved traveling on the weekends to her grandparents'	13
house in Connecticut was her Grandpa Bob. As soon as she and her parents pulled	28
into the winding drive and stopped in front of her grandparents' house, she and	42
Grandpa Bob would go for a walk.	49
Becky lived in New York City in an apartment she shared with her parents and a	65
golden retriever named Ralph. She and Ralph walked in the city, and she saw lots	80
of interesting things. They saw yellow taxicabs, men in suits, and women in high	94
heels. But never in New York did she see the fantastic things she saw with Grandpa	110
Bob on their walks.	114
Grandpa Bob knew just about everything there was to know about the forest and	128
the animals that lived there. Once, when she and Grandpa Bob were walking, a	142
blue bird landed on his shoulder. When it flew away, Becky remembered her	155
grandpa had looked down at her and winked.	163
"It was just telling me some secrets, that's all, Becky," he had told her. "That bird	179
just told me there would be a frost tonight and that there is a herd of deer nibbling on	198
grass just beyond those maple trees."	204
Becky followed with her eyes where her grandpa was pointing and saw a pelt of	219
brown fur and the long legs and the velvet nose that did indeed belong to a white-	236
tailed deer.	238
She couldn't believe a blue bird was smart enough to tell her grandpa all that. At	254
the same time, she wished one of those critters would land on her shoulder and sing	270
secrets to her.	273
Later that evening, when Grandpa Bob was dozing in front of the fire with his	288
pipe hanging out of his mouth and Becky and her mom and dad were playing a	304
game of cards with Grandma, Becky leaned in close to her mom and whispered in	319
her ear.	321
"When I grow up Mom, I think I'm going to be like Grandpa Bob."	335

TIMING THE READING

A bracket indicates where the student stopped at the one-minute mark.

SCORE	141	–	3	=	138
	words attempted in one minute		number of errors		words correct per minute (wcpm)

Grade 6 | TEACHER COPY: Benchmark Fluency Passage #1   19

Teacher Version, Grade 6 Benchmark Fluency Passage #1

Reporting Results

Benchmark Assessments

Plot each of the three scores, and then write the median (middle) score in the box at the bottom of the form. Compare the student's score to the grade-level norm for the time of year (printed at bottom and also shown on the graph as dark lines). Use the beginning-of-the-year data to set improvement goals and plan instruction; use the mid- and end-of-year data to evaluate progress and instructional effectiveness.

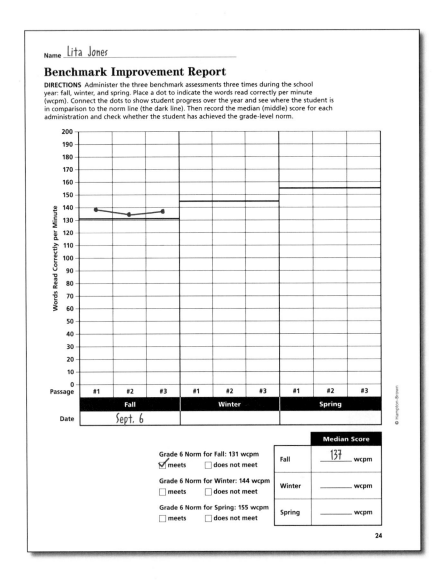

Progress Monitoring Assessments

Use the student's Benchmark Assessment results and the expected ROI (rate of improvement) for the student's grade-level reading ability to set goals and measure progress toward those goals weekly.

1. Draw a goal line in pencil for a grading period.
2. Mark a dot for wcpm on each weekly assessment.
3. Compare to the goal in order to determine whether instruction needs to be adjusted or whether a more challenging goal needs to be set. (Mark a vertical line to show the date of any instructional intervention so that you can judge its effect.)
4. Finally, connect the dots to show progress over the year.

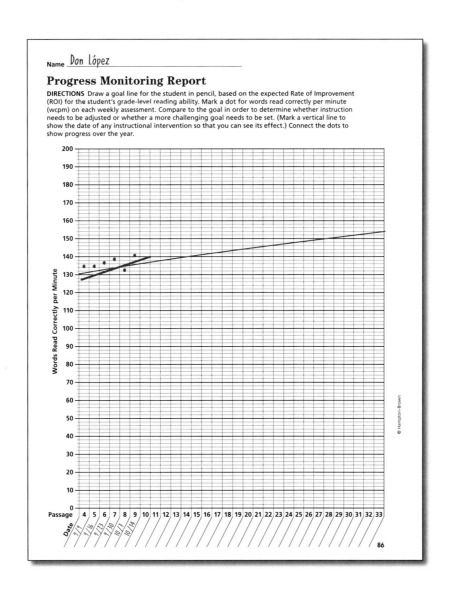

Improving Reading Fluency

Students become fluent readers by reading—and rereading—texts that are within their instructional range. Here are some instructional strategies to incorporate into your literacy time to enhance fluency.

Oral Reading Modeling

Expose students regularly to models of fluent reading, either by reading aloud to them yourself or using recorded story readings. This helps students learn how and when a reader pauses and changes tone and pitch for expression.

Phrasing

Type a passage from the beginning of a story that is within students' instructional reading level. Include an extra line space between each line of text (i.e., double spaced). Read aloud the passage with fluency while students listen and use slashes to mark where they hear pauses. Have them use one slash for short pauses (as between phrases)and two slashes for longer pauses (as between sentences). Then have them use their marked sheets to practice reading aloud to a partner with appropriate phrasing.

Repeated Reading

Reading the same text over again doesn't have to be boring! Encourage younger students to partner-read decodable text and older students to read aloud to younger ones. During classroom discussions, have students read aloud a passage from the textbook or story to support their answers.

Readers Theater

Make Readers Theater a regular part of your classroom routine. Choose stories that have simple plots plus a good amount of dialog. After you choose a narrator and assign character parts to students, have each of them practice their parts every day for a week. (Note that students should not attempt to memorize the text.) During rehearsal, encourage students to give each other feedback about rate, phrasing, intonation, and expression.

Reading Growth Across the Grades

If you have students whose reading levels are significantly above or below grade-level norms, use the Grades 1–8 data in this table to find norms and expected ROI (rate of improvement).

Reading Growth Grades 1–8

	Fall			Winter			Spring			
	Number of Students	Percentile	Words Read Correctly	Number of Students	Percentile	Words Read Correctly	Number of Students	Percentile	Words Read Correctly	ROI
Grade 1	6,087	90	42	28,842	90	74	30,511	90	104	1.7
		75	19		75	44		75	78	1.6
		50	7		50	23		50	50	1.2
		25	2		25	12		25	27	0.7
		10	0		10	6		10	14	0.4
Grade 2	25,620	90	100	27,649	90	126	28,226	90	143	1.2
		75	75		75	101		75	117	1.2
		50	51		50	75		50	91	1.1
		25	24		25	50		25	67	1.2
		10	13		10	24		10	39	0.7
Grade 3	23,857	90	130	26,420	90	147	27,101	90	163	0.9
		75	102		75	122		75	138	1
		50	75		50	94		50	110	1
		25	47		25	65		25	81	0.9
		10	28		10	39		10	51	0.6
Grade 4	21,877	90	148	23,067	90	167	23,886	90	183	1
		75	122		75	140		75	154	0.9
		50	98		50	113		50	125	0.8
		25	72		25	89		25	100	0.8
		10	47		10	62		10	72	0.7
Grade 5	20,920	90	168	22,038	90	182	22,869	90	198	0.8
		75	140		75	156		75	171	0.9
		50	111		50	126		50	140	0.8
		25	84		25	98		25	108	0.7
		10	59		10	73		10	81	0.6
Grade 6	15,236	90	181	15,584	90	198	16,954	90	211	0.8
		75	158		75	170		75	183	0.7
		50	131		50	144		50	155	0.7
		25	101		25	113		25	125	0.7
		10	70		10	83		10	94	0.7
Grade 7	8,187	90	184	7,479	90	197	9,526	90	208	0.7
		75	158		75	170		75	182	0.7
		50	131		50	140		50	154	0.6
		25	104		25	114		25	125	0.6
		10	82		10	89		10	99	0.5
Grade 8	6,233	90	185	6,027	90	194	7,740	90	200	0.4
		75	163		75	171		75	180	0.5
		50	140		50	148		50	156	0.4
		25	109		25	117		25	129	0.6
		10	78		10	86		10	98	0.6

Benchmark
Passages

One of the reasons Becky loved traveling on the weekends to her grandparents' house in Connecticut was her Grandpa Bob. As soon as she and her parents pulled into the winding drive and stopped in front of her grandparents' house, she and Grandpa Bob would go for a walk.

Becky lived in New York City in an apartment she shared with her parents and a golden retriever named Ralph. She and Ralph walked in the city, and she saw lots of interesting things. They saw yellow taxicabs, men in suits, and women in high heels. But never in New York did she see the fantastic things she saw with Grandpa Bob on their walks.

Grandpa Bob knew just about everything there was to know about the forest and the animals that lived there. Once, when she and Grandpa Bob were walking, a blue bird landed on his shoulder. When it flew away, Becky remembered her grandpa had looked down at her and winked.

"It was just telling me some secrets, that's all, Becky," he had told her. "That bird just told me there would be a frost tonight and that there is a herd of deer nibbling on grass just beyond those maple trees."

Becky followed with her eyes where her grandpa was pointing and saw a pelt of brown fur and the long legs and the velvet nose that did indeed belong to a white-tailed deer.

She couldn't believe a blue bird was smart enough to tell her grandpa all that. At the same time, she wished one of those critters would land on her shoulder and sing secrets to her.

Later that evening, when Grandpa Bob was dozing in front of the fire with his pipe hanging out of his mouth and Becky and her mom and dad were playing a game of cards with Grandma, Becky leaned in close to her mom and whispered in her ear.

"When I grow up Mom, I think I'm going to be like Grandpa Bob."

One of the reasons Becky loved traveling on the weekends to her grandparents'   13

house in Connecticut was her Grandpa Bob. As soon as she and her parents pulled   28

into the winding drive and stopped in front of her grandparents' house, she and   42

Grandpa Bob would go for a walk.   49

    Becky lived in New York City in an apartment she shared with her parents and a   65

golden retriever named Ralph. She and Ralph walked in the city, and she saw lots   80

of interesting things. They saw yellow taxicabs, men in suits, and women in high   94

heels. But never in New York did she see the fantastic things she saw with Grandpa   110

Bob on their walks.   114

    Grandpa Bob knew just about everything there was to know about the forest and   128

the animals that lived there. Once, when she and Grandpa Bob were walking, a   142

blue bird landed on his shoulder. When it flew away, Becky remembered her   155

grandpa had looked down at her and winked.   163

    "It was just telling me some secrets, that's all, Becky," he had told her. "That bird   179

just told me there would be a frost tonight and that there is a herd of deer nibbling on   198

grass just beyond those maple trees."   204

    Becky followed with her eyes where her grandpa was pointing and saw a pelt of   219

brown fur and the long legs and the velvet nose that did indeed belong to a white-   236

tailed deer.   238

    She couldn't believe a blue bird was smart enough to tell her grandpa all that. At   254

the same time, she wished one of those critters would land on her shoulder and sing   270

secrets to her.   273

    Later that evening, when Grandpa Bob was dozing in front of the fire with his   288

pipe hanging out of his mouth and Becky and her mom and dad were playing a   304

game of cards with Grandma, Becky leaned in close to her mom and whispered in   319

her ear.   321

    "When I grow up Mom, I think I'm going to be like Grandpa Bob."   335

SCORE	_____	−	_____	=	_____
	words attempted in one minute		number of errors		words correct per minute (wcpm)

I was terrified. When my mom climbed out of the car and started walking toward the dentist's office, I stayed where I was, shivering in the front passenger seat of our car. Then, on a stroke of pure genius, I hit the button on the side control panel that locked all the doors on the vehicle at once. I wasn't going in there. I didn't care if I had crooked teeth for the rest of my life. Do you know what they do to you in dentist offices?

I found out last night while talking on the telephone with my best friend Marcy, who got braces last year. She told me that first they strap you down in the chair, and then they whip out the drills they've been hiding behind their backs. They have to SCREW on each brace, and they only give you the tiniest bit of painkillers. Then they get out the metal wires and tighten and pull to their hearts' content.

Marcy also told me her dentist, Dr. Pane, pulled so hard all of her teeth fell out. She told me it had taken Dr. Pane five hours to glue her teeth back in place. I think Marcy may be stretching the truth a little, but I know some of what lies ahead of me will, no doubt, cause me great bodily harm.

My mom raps sharply on the window.

"Let's go, Gloria," she says.

I get out of the car because she has the keys in her purse anyway, and I don't want to look like an idiot because my mother had to carry me over her shoulder kicking and screaming to get my braces put on.

"You know you're very lucky," my mom tells me as we walk up the sidewalk. "I wanted braces when I was your age, but I couldn't have them."

I don't say anything.

My mom pulls open the door and then steps aside, letting another woman and her son walk out. The boy smiles at me. His teeth are strapped with metal.

I pinch my lips over my tilted teeth, blushing. I can't wait until I get my braces on.

I was terrified. When my mom climbed out of the car and started walking toward   15

the dentist's office, I stayed where I was, shivering in the front passenger seat of our   31

car. Then, on a stroke of pure genius, I hit the button on the side control panel that   49

locked all the doors on the vehicle at once. I wasn't going in there. I didn't care if I   68

had crooked teeth for the rest of my life. Do you know what they do to you in dentist   87

offices?   88

I found out last night while talking on the telephone with my best friend Marcy,   103

who got braces last year. She told me that first they strap you down in the chair,   120

and then they whip out the drills they've been hiding behind their backs. They have   135

to SCREW on each brace, and they only give you the tiniest bit of painkillers. Then   151

they get out the metal wires and tighten and pull to their hearts' content.   165

Marcy also told me her dentist, Dr. Pane, pulled so hard all of her teeth fell out.   182

She told me it had taken Dr. Pane five hours to glue her teeth back in place. I think   201

Marcy may be stretching the truth a little, but I know some of what lies ahead of me   219

will, no doubt, cause me great bodily harm.   227

My mom raps sharply on the window.   234

"Let's go, Gloria," she says.   239

I get out of the car because she has the keys in her purse anyway, and I don't   257

want to look like an idiot because my mother had to carry me over her shoulder   273

kicking and screaming to get my braces put on.   282

"You know you're very lucky," my mom tells me as we walk up the sidewalk. "I   298

wanted braces when I was your age, but I couldn't have them."   310

I don't say anything.   314

My mom pulls open the door and then steps aside, letting another woman and   328

her son walk out. The boy smiles at me. His teeth are strapped with metal.   343

I pinch my lips over my tilted teeth, blushing. I can't wait until I get my braces on.   361

SCORE	_____	−	_____	=	_____
	words attempted in one minute		number of errors		words correct per minute (wcpm)

The land outside the hunting grounds of Black Raven's tribe was beautiful and filled with wild game and tall trees. Unfortunately, no one would brave the rapids of the Silver River to get to it. As a result, Black Raven's family and friends were running out of food.

The Silver River twisted through a mountain pass on the edge of the tribe's territory. The stone cliffs of the mountain pass were sharp and steep, and no one could climb them. The only way out of the valley was on the river, but sadly, no one was daring—or reckless—enough to brave the untamed water.

Many young men in the tribe boasted that some day they would ride the river to the other side of the mountains and into the fertile valley. They bragged around the campfires as they ate the last of the silver trout from the Silver River.

One evening the old wise man of the tribe interrupted the young men's talk and spoke. "The time has come," he said, "for someone to journey beyond our lands. Who is brave enough to ride the river?"

Many of the young men around the fire jumped up without thinking. Some of them couldn't even swim, but they raised their hands just the same and shouted out that they would surely beat the river and become heroes.

Black Raven was the only young man to stay seated. He thought quietly as the other men strutted and swaggered. He thought about what kind of vessel he would need to float on top of the water and avoid the sharp rocks of the rapids, and as he thought, he reached out and fingered the silvery bark of one of the birch trees nearest to him. He peeled a bit off the tree and thought it just might work.

"What of you, Black Raven?" one of the arrogant boys called out. "Are you too frightened to take on the river?"

"No," Black Raven said as he stood. "I think I have an idea that might work. Come, let us sit and think this over."

The land outside the hunting grounds of Black Raven's tribe was beautiful and   13

filled with wild game and tall trees. Unfortunately, no one would brave the rapids of   28

the Silver River to get to it. As a result, Black Raven's family and friends were   44

running out of food.   48

The Silver River twisted through a mountain pass on the edge of the tribe's   62

territory. The stone cliffs of the mountain pass were sharp and steep, and no one   77

could climb them. The only way out of the valley was on the river, but sadly, no one   95

was daring—or reckless—enough to brave the untamed water.   105

Many young men in the tribe boasted that some day they would ride the river to   121

the other side of the mountains and into the fertile valley. They bragged around the   136

campfires as they ate the last of the silver trout from the Silver River.   150

One evening the old wise man of the tribe interrupted the young men's talk and   165

spoke. "The time has come," he said, "for someone to journey beyond our lands.   179

Who is brave enough to ride the river?"   187

Many of the young men around the fire jumped up without thinking. Some of   201

them couldn't even swim, but they raised their hands just the same and shouted out   216

that they would surely beat the river and become heroes.   226

Black Raven was the only young man to stay seated. He thought quietly as the   241

other men strutted and swaggered. He thought about what kind of vessel he would   255

need to float on top of the water and avoid the sharp rocks of the rapids, and as he   274

thought, he reached out and fingered the silvery bark of one of the birch trees   289

nearest to him. He peeled a bit off the tree and thought it just might work.   305

"What of you, Black Raven?" one of the arrogant boys called out. "Are you too   320

frightened to take on the river?"   326

"No," Black Raven said as he stood. "I think I have an idea that might work.   342

Come, let us sit and think this over."   350

SCORE	_____	−	_____	=	_____
	words attempted in one minute		number of errors		words correct per minute (wcpm)

Benchmark Improvement Report

DIRECTIONS Administer the three benchmark assessments three times during the school year: fall, winter, and spring. Place a dot to indicate the words read correctly per minute (wcpm). Connect the dots to show student progress over the year and see where the student is in comparison to the norm line (the dark line). Then record the median (middle) score for each administration and check whether the student has achieved the grade-level norm.

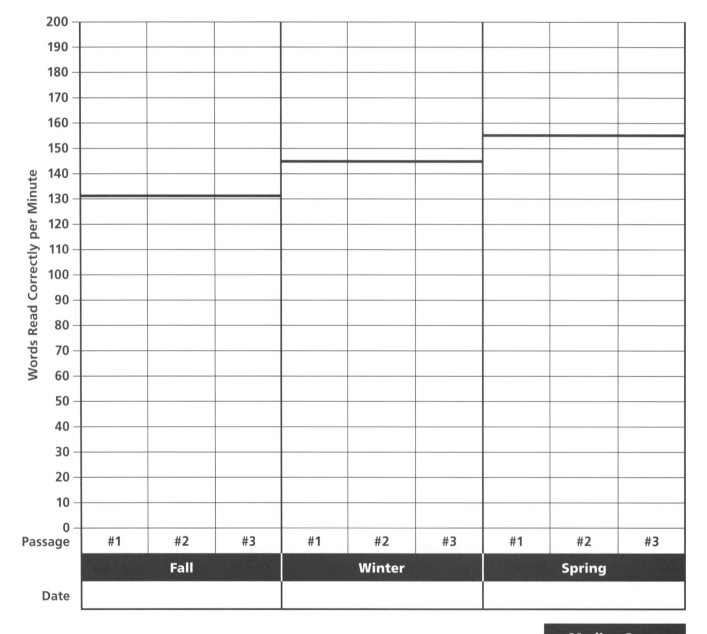

Grade 6 Norm for Fall: 131 wcpm
☐ meets   ☐ does not meet

Grade 6 Norm for Winter: 144 wcpm
☐ meets   ☐ does not meet

Grade 6 Norm for Spring: 155 wcpm
☐ meets   ☐ does not meet

	Median Score
Fall	_____ wcpm
Winter	_____ wcpm
Spring	_____ wcpm

Progress Monitoring Passages

Hundreds of years ago, in a land far away, an old man named Alexander rescued helpless children. Alexander had a very kind heart. He didn't want the children to go without food, clothing, or shelter. Alexander often drove his mule-drawn wagon around the town searching for homeless children to help.

On this particular day, Alexander drove his wagon through a very poor village. He saw a little boy and a little girl sitting in an alley. Their clothes were torn, and the children were very dirty. They sat close together and cried.

"Why are you crying?" asked Alexander from atop his wagon.

"Our mother and father have died. We have no family and nothing to eat," said the little girl.

"We are hungry," said the little boy. "Can you help us, Sir?"

Alexander told the little boy and girl to climb into his wagon. Alexander took the little boy and girl to his farm in the country. At the farm, they saw dozens of other children busy at work. Out in the field, young boys were cutting down hay. In the barn, young girls were milking cows.

"All of these children have lost their parents," Alexander told the little boy and girl. "We all work together so we can eat and keep the farmhouse clean. I find good homes with loving mothers and fathers for most of the boys and girls. I will find a good home for you too. But until we find a good home for you, I must teach you how to work so you can help us keep ourselves fed."

The boy and girl were more than happy to work. The little boy ran out into the fields to work with the other boys. The boys were kind and helpful. They taught the little boy how to use a pitchfork. The girl offered to help with the cooking and the dishes. The little boy and girl were very happy in their new home.

Hundreds of years ago, in a land far away, an old man named Alexander rescued   15
helpless children. Alexander had a very kind heart. He didn't want the children to   29
go without food, clothing, or shelter. Alexander often drove his mule-drawn wagon   42
around the town searching for homeless children to help.   51

On this particular day, Alexander drove his wagon through a very poor village.   64
He saw a little boy and a little girl sitting in an alley. Their clothes were torn, and the   83
children were very dirty. They sat close together and cried.   93

"Why are you crying?" asked Alexander from atop his wagon.   103

"Our mother and father have died. We have no family and nothing to eat," said   118
the little girl.   121

"We are hungry," said the little boy. "Can you help us, Sir?"   133

Alexander told the little boy and girl to climb into his wagon. Alexander took the   148
little boy and girl to his farm in the country. At the farm, they saw dozens of other   166
children busy at work. Out in the field, young boys were cutting down hay. In the   182
barn, young girls were milking cows.   188

"All of these children have lost their parents," Alexander told the little boy and girl.   203
"We all work together so we can eat and keep the farmhouse clean. I find good   219
homes with loving mothers and fathers for most of the boys and girls. I will find a   236
good home for you too. But until we find a good home for you, I must teach you how   255
to work so you can help us keep ourselves fed."   265

The boy and girl were more than happy to work. The little boy ran out into the   282
fields to work with the other boys. The boys were kind and helpful. They taught the   298
little boy how to use a pitchfork. The girl offered to help with the cooking and the   315
dishes. The little boy and girl were very happy in their new home.   328

SCORE	_____	−	_____	=	_____
	words attempted in one minute		number of errors		words correct per minute (wcpm)

Beatrice hated books. Books were dusty and musty and filled with long, tangled sentences that made no sense—at least not to Beatrice. Books were heavy and clumsy and so boring that whenever Beatrice sat herself down and forced herself to read, she fell right to sleep.

One stormy evening, Beatrice was sitting in the library doing nothing when her mother looked in on her.

"Beatrice, darling," she said, "why don't you read a book?"

"All the books in here are boring," she told her mother.

"They are not," her mother shouted. "You will read a book, and you will give me a full report in the morning." Then she stormed out of the room.

Beatrice was so angry she kicked the wall and screamed twice. She screamed the first time because she'd stubbed her toe and the second time because a book had become dislodged from the shelf above and fallen on her head.

The book fell open on the floor at her feet. A few stray wisps of sparkling dust rose from its moldy pages, tickling Beatrice's nose and causing her to sneeze.

"Bless you."

The voice came from the shadows all around Beatrice. She heard a faint chuckle as she narrowed her eyes and looked from side to side. No one was there. Beatrice knew she was alone with the book, so who had spoken to her?

"I did, you fool."

The voice came again, louder this time, and Beatrice finally looked down at her feet realizing that it was the book that spoke. Beatrice tried to close the cover of the book with her toe.

"That won't work," said the book, now ruffling its pages because it was upset. "I don't like to be kicked. Books should be treated with respect. Let me show you something."

The book ruffled its pages once more, and a strong wind blew as the pages turned. Finally, the book stopped on a page with a picture of a trapdoor. The handle of the trapdoor gleamed.

"Go ahead," said the book. "Pull it open. A world of adventure awaits you, young Beatrice."

Beatrice hated books. Books were dusty and musty and filled with long, tangled   13

sentences that made no sense—at least not to Beatrice. Books were heavy and   27

clumsy and so boring that whenever Beatrice sat herself down and forced herself to   41

read, she fell right to sleep.   47

One stormy evening, Beatrice was sitting in the library doing nothing when her   60

mother looked in on her.   65

"Beatrice, darling," she said, "why don't you read a book?"   75

"All the books in here are boring," she told her mother.   86

"They are not," her mother shouted. "You will read a book, and you will give me a   103

full report in the morning." Then she stormed out of the room.   115

Beatrice was so angry she kicked the wall and screamed twice. She screamed   128

the first time because she'd stubbed her toe and the second time because a book had   144

become dislodged from the shelf above and fallen on her head.   155

The book fell open on the floor at her feet. A few stray wisps of sparkling dust   172

rose from its moldy pages, tickling Beatrice's nose and causing her to sneeze.   185

"Bless you."   187

The voice came from the shadows all around Beatrice. She heard a faint chuckle   201

as she narrowed her eyes and looked from side to side. No one was there. Beatrice   217

knew she was alone with the book, so who had spoken to her?   230

"I did, you fool."   234

The voice came again, louder this time, and Beatrice finally looked down at her   248

feet realizing that it was the book that spoke. Beatrice tried to close the cover of the   265

book with her toe.   269

"That won't work," said the book, now ruffling its pages because it was upset. "I   284

don't like to be kicked. Books should be treated with respect. Let me show you   299

something."   300

The book ruffled its pages once more, and a strong wind blew as the pages   315

turned. Finally, the book stopped on a page with a picture of a trapdoor. The handle   331

of the trapdoor gleamed.   335

"Go ahead," said the book. "Pull it open. A world of adventure awaits you, young   350

Beatrice."   351

SCORE	_____	−	_____	=	_____
	words attempted in one minute		number of errors		words correct per minute (wcpm)

Crystal's next door neighbor was a very large and strange man. He was well over six feet tall with feet the size of tennis rackets. Sometimes while riding the bus to school, Crystal saw him at the dump digging through piles of garbage. Sometimes while riding the bus home from school, she saw him walking down the sidewalk lugging a heavy burlap sack over his shoulder. Crystal never knew what was in the sack. She could only guess as she watched him open his front door and close it behind him. Her older brother, Jason, had an idea.

"Maybe the guy next door is so poor," he told Crystal one afternoon, "he has to go to the dump to scavenge for food. I bet he collects old boots and makes boot-leather soup." Crystal wrinkled her nose. She didn't like the sound of that.

"Do you think I should bring him some food?" she asked. "I could bring him some of the leftover cinnamon rolls Mom made last weekend." Jason was too busy laughing to answer. Crystal ignored her big brother. She knew he could be rude and mean sometimes.

The next morning before school, Crystal walked across the yard and knocked on her neighbor's front door. She knocked several times, but no one answered. Crystal left the tray of cinnamon rolls covered with tinfoil on his steps and ran to catch the bus. She didn't see the curtains twitch as she turned to leave, but she did see piles of rusty old pipes stacked in the backyard.

All day as Crystal sat in class, she wondered what her neighbor used those pipes for. When she got home, she found a clean plate and a folded piece of tinfoil on her front steps. She ran across her yard to her neighbor's door.

Before she could knock, the door opened. Her neighbor stood in the doorway towering over her. Crystal would have been scared to death had there not been a kind smile on his face and a sincere look in his eyes. He didn't say a word. Instead he handed her a beautiful set of silver wind chimes.

"How lovely," she said. "Thank you very much." Crystal now understood what her neighbor did with his burlap sack and his backyard full of pipes.

Crystal's next door neighbor was a very large and strange man. He was well	14
over six feet tall with feet the size of tennis rackets. Sometimes while riding the bus	30
to school, Crystal saw him at the dump digging through piles of garbage.	43
Sometimes while riding the bus home from school, she saw him walking down the	57
sidewalk lugging a heavy burlap sack over his shoulder. Crystal never knew what	70
was in the sack. She could only guess as she watched him open his front door and	87
close it behind him. Her older brother, Jason, had an idea.	98
"Maybe the guy next door is so poor," he told Crystal one afternoon, "he has to	114
go to the dump to scavenge for food. I bet he collects old boots and makes boot-	131
leather soup." Crystal wrinkled her nose. She didn't like the sound of that.	144
"Do you think I should bring him some food?" she asked. "I could bring him	159
some of the leftover cinnamon rolls Mom made last weekend." Jason was too busy	173
laughing to answer. Crystal ignored her big brother. She knew he could be rude	187
and mean sometimes.	190
The next morning before school, Crystal walked across the yard and knocked on	203
her neighbor's front door. She knocked several times, but no one answered. Crystal	216
left the tray of cinnamon rolls covered with tinfoil on his steps and ran to catch the	233
bus. She didn't see the curtains twitch as she turned to leave, but she did see piles	250
of rusty old pipes stacked in the backyard.	258
All day as Crystal sat in class, she wondered what her neighbor used those pipes	273
for. When she got home, she found a clean plate and a folded piece of tinfoil on her	291
front steps. She ran across her yard to her neighbor's door.	302
Before she could knock, the door opened. Her neighbor stood in the doorway	315
towering over her. Crystal would have been scared to death had there not been a	330
kind smile on his face and a sincere look in his eyes. He didn't say a word. Instead	348
he handed her a beautiful set of silver wind chimes.	358
"How lovely," she said. "Thank you very much." Crystal now understood what	370
her neighbor did with his burlap sack and his backyard full of pipes.	383

SCORE	_____	−	_____	=	_____
	words attempted in one minute		number of errors		words correct per minute (wcpm)

Mr. Lee thought his dog, Little Lee, was the smartest dog on the block. Little Lee brought Mr. Lee his paper and slippers every morning and his glasses and word find book every evening. Little Lee could sit, speak, stay, and shake. He could open doors and turn lights on and off. Little Lee could even howl Mr. Lee's favorite songs.

When Mr. Lee began to lose his sight a few years ago, Little Lee began leading Mr. Lee around whenever Mr. Lee put him on his leash. Little Lee watched Mr. Lee's every step. He knew red lights meant stop and green lights meant go. He helped Mr. Lee cross streets, get on elevators, and shop for groceries. He had a knack for picking out the tenderest pieces of steak and pork chops at the meat market.

In the mornings, Mr. Lee always took Little Lee for a walk. Sometimes they would go to the park and Mr. Lee would let Little Lee off his leash. After the park, they would walk down the street a bit further to the ice cream stand. Mr. Lee always had chocolate chip, and Little Lee always had French vanilla. Then Mr. Lee would follow his trusty dog all the way home.

One night over a dinner of steak and baked potatoes, Mr. Lee spoke to his dog. "Little Lee, you are not only the smartest dog on the block, but I think you are the smartest dog in the neighborhood. In fact you're probably the smartest dog in the entire city." Little Lee wagged his tail as he cracked a bone between his teeth. He barked twice to let Mr. Lee know that he understood him.

That night while Mr. Lee watched a little television, Little Lee slept snuggled on the couch beside him. Mr. Lee scratched Little Lee in all the right places. He scratched Little Lee behind his ears, between his shoulder blades, and up and down his furry tummy. As always, Little Lee fell asleep with his head on Mr. Lee's lap.

Mr. Lee thought his dog, Little Lee, was the smartest dog on the block. Little Lee   16
brought Mr. Lee his paper and slippers every morning and his glasses and word find   31
book every evening. Little Lee could sit, speak, stay, and shake. He could open   45
doors and turn lights on and off. Little Lee could even howl Mr. Lee's favorite songs.   61

When Mr. Lee began to lose his sight a few years ago, Little Lee began leading   77
Mr. Lee around whenever Mr. Lee put him on his leash. Little Lee watched Mr. Lee's   93
every step. He knew red lights meant stop and green lights meant go. He helped   108
Mr. Lee cross streets, get on elevators, and shop for groceries. He had a knack for   124
picking out the tenderest pieces of steak and pork chops at the meat market.   138

In the mornings, Mr. Lee always took Little Lee for a walk. Sometimes they   152
would go to the park and Mr. Lee would let Little Lee off his leash. After the park,   170
they would walk down the street a bit further to the ice cream stand. Mr. Lee always   187
had chocolate chip, and Little Lee always had French vanilla. Then Mr. Lee would   201
follow his trusty dog all the way home.   209

One night over a dinner of steak and baked potatoes, Mr. Lee spoke to his dog.   225
"Little Lee, you are not only the smartest dog on the block, but I think you are the   243
smartest dog in the neighborhood. In fact you're probably the smartest dog in the   257
entire city." Little Lee wagged his tail as he cracked a bone between his teeth. He   273
barked twice to let Mr. Lee know that he understood him.   284

That night while Mr. Lee watched a little television, Little Lee slept snuggled on   298
the couch beside him. Mr. Lee scratched Little Lee in all the right places. He   313
scratched Little Lee behind his ears, between his shoulder blades, and up and down   327
his furry tummy. As always, Little Lee fell asleep with his head on Mr. Lee's lap.   343

SCORE   _____ − _____ = _____
words attempted   number of errors   words correct per
in one minute   minute (wcpm)

Fall is my favorite season. I love to watch the leaves change color and flutter to the ground on cool, crisp fall days. All of my fondest memories seem to involve fall.

One of my favorite memories happened around a campfire last October. My cousins from Nebraska had come to visit us, and we spent the afternoon gathering firewood and preparing the area for a campfire. After dinner, everyone walked down the path to the beachfront where we had set up a pile of logs for the fire. It was almost dark, and we could barely see each other's faces.

"Isn't someone going to light the fire?" asked my Uncle Milton.

"Be patient. The children have a plan," said my mother.

My cousin Sarah waited for everyone to be quiet then she lit a match. The crumpled newspaper caught fire and within seconds, flames rose into the air.

Uncle Milton let out a high-pitched shriek and took a step backwards. As he stepped back, he stumbled over something behind him, lost his footing, and landed with a splash in a bucket of water.

My cousins and I took one look at Uncle Milton and began to laugh. One by one, the adults began laughing until Uncle Milton was the only one who wasn't laughing. Then, a smile slowly spread across his face, and soon he was laughing harder than any of us.

"May I ask where that bucket of water came from?" he said when the laughter had died down.

"I filled it and brought it here this afternoon in case the fire got away from us," said my cousin Chip. "You should have expected us to use that kind of caution, Dad. You're a firefighter, remember?" he asked. Uncle Milton was the fire chief in his hometown.

"Well, aren't you just a chip off the old block," said my uncle, and everyone started laughing all over again.

Fall is my favorite season. I love to watch the leaves change color and flutter to   16

the ground on cool, crisp fall days. All of my fondest memories seem to involve fall.   32

One of my favorite memories happened around a campfire last October. My   44

cousins from Nebraska had come to visit us, and we spent the afternoon gathering   58

firewood and preparing the area for a campfire. After dinner, everyone walked down   71

the path to the beachfront where we had set up a pile of logs for the fire. It was   90

almost dark, and we could barely see each other's faces.   100

"Isn't someone going to light the fire?" asked my Uncle Milton.   111

"Be patient. The children have a plan," said my mother.   121

My cousin Sarah waited for everyone to be quiet then she lit a match.   135

The crumpled newspaper caught fire and within seconds, flames rose into the air.   148

Uncle Milton let out a high-pitched shriek and took a step backwards. As he   162

stepped back, he stumbled over something behind him, lost his footing, and landed   175

with a splash in a bucket of water.   183

My cousins and I took one look at Uncle Milton and began to laugh. One by one,   200

the adults began laughing until Uncle Milton was the only one who wasn't laughing.   214

Then, a smile slowly spread across his face, and soon he was laughing harder than   229

any of us.   232

"May I ask where that bucket of water came from?" he said when the laughter had   248

died down.   250

"I filled it and brought it here this afternoon in case the fire got away from us," said   268

my cousin Chip. "You should have expected us to use that kind of caution, Dad.   283

You're a firefighter, remember?" he asked. Uncle Milton was the fire chief in his   297

hometown.   298

"Well, aren't you just a chip off the old block," said my uncle, and everyone started   314

laughing all over again.   318

SCORE	_____	−	_____	=	_____
	words attempted in one minute		number of errors		words correct per minute (wcpm)

Every day after school all the kids flocked to Jim's house to play computer games. They knew that Jim was the best player in the school, maybe even in town. Nobody could beat Jim at any computer game, but they always tried.

One afternoon Jim was playing Space Ace with his friends. He played very well that day and reached a championship level of performance. His score was higher than anyone in history. He took a picture of the screen and mailed it into the company that created the game.

Two months later, while Jim and his friends were playing games, the doorbell rang. Jim's mother answered the door, and there stood two men in uniforms. They were from NASA, and they wanted to speak to Jim. "Jimmy, come here," said his mother. Jim stopped playing and ran to the door. He was surprised to see men from NASA standing there.

The men explained to Jim that they had seen the picture of his high score in Space Ace and wanted to know if he would help them. There had been an accident in space, and some astronauts were in trouble. The only hope of reaching them was to send a remote controlled rocket into space. There was no time to test the remote controlled rocket. NASA needed Jim to fly the rocket for them right away.

Jim was more surprised than before. "Yes! I'll help if I can," said Jim. Jim and his mother flew to NASA in Florida. There was no time to waste. Jim sat in the pilot seat. The rocket took off. Jim controlled the rocket's flight through space. It was just like the computer game! He flew the rocket around planets and moons. He saw many small asteroids ahead of him. He fired the guns to destroy space rocks and flew quickly to reach the space station. Finally, Jim saw the space station in the distance and flew at super speed. He docked perfectly with the space station. Jim had saved the astronauts, and NASA was very thankful. Jim's picture was in newspapers around the world.

Every day after school all the kids flocked to Jim's house to play computer	14
games. They knew that Jim was the best player in the school, maybe even in town.	30
Nobody could beat Jim at any computer game, but they always tried.	42
One afternoon Jim was playing Space Ace with his friends. He played very well	56
that day and reached a championship level of performance. His score was higher	69
than anyone in history. He took a picture of the screen and mailed it into the	85
company that created the game.	90
Two months later, while Jim and his friends were playing games, the doorbell	103
rang. Jim's mother answered the door, and there stood two men in uniforms. They	117
were from NASA, and they wanted to speak to Jim. "Jimmy, come here," said his	132
mother. Jim stopped playing and ran to the door. He was surprised to see men	147
from NASA standing there.	151
The men explained to Jim that they had seen the picture of his high score in	167
Space Ace and wanted to know if he would help them. There had been an accident	183
in space, and some astronauts were in trouble. The only hope of reaching them was	198
to send a remote controlled rocket into space. There was no time to test the remote	214
controlled rocket. NASA needed Jim to fly the rocket for them right away.	227
Jim was more surprised than before. "Yes! I'll help if I can," said Jim. Jim and	243
his mother flew to NASA in Florida. There was no time to waste. Jim sat in the pilot	261
seat. The rocket took off. Jim controlled the rocket's flight through space. It was	275
just like the computer game! He flew the rocket around planets and moons. He saw	290
many small asteroids ahead of him. He fired the guns to destroy space rocks and	305
flew quickly to reach the space station. Finally, Jim saw the space station in the	320
distance and flew at super speed. He docked perfectly with the space station. Jim	334
had saved the astronauts, and NASA was very thankful. Jim's picture was in	347
newspapers around the world.	351

SCORE	_____	–	_____	=	_____
	words attempted in one minute		number of errors		words correct per minute (wcpm)

© Edformation, Inc.

I must be the only ten-year-old kid in the universe who has a time-travel machine. I began to use it just yesterday. My time-travel machine has a wide variety of buttons. Yesterday I got in, closed my eyes, and pressed one of the buttons. When I opened my eyes and looked out, I found myself in Ancient Egypt! I peered out the window and saw warriors running towards me. They looked angry, so I pressed a button that said "The Future" and quickly arrived back at my house.

I decided the time-travel machine was way cool and called my best friends, Jeff and Justin. I didn't tell them about the time-travel machine over the phone because I knew they wouldn't believe me. They always questioned the things I told them.

A few minutes later, I looked out my bedroom window. Sure enough, Jeff and Justin were walking up the driveway. "Hey," I said. "You guys have to see the time machine I found."

"You know we're too old for make-believe," Justin said as he folded his arms.

"No, I'm serious," I insisted, leading them to my machine. With their eyes wide open, they stood in complete silence. After a lot of questions, they convinced me they were ready to try it out. We crammed into the machine, and I randomly pressed one of the buttons. Suddenly we found ourselves in medieval England. Jeff and Justin were totally amazed. They couldn't believe their eyes! Just as we were about to step out, we noticed several knights in shining armor approaching. I decided not to chance it. I hit the future button, and we ended up safe and sound back in my home.

Jeff and Justin made me promise to take them on another adventure very soon. Hopefully, next time we will be able to stay longer and explore more of the past.

I must be the only ten-year-old kid in the universe who has a time-travel machine. 18

I began to use it just yesterday. My time-travel machine has a wide variety of 34

buttons. Yesterday I got in, closed my eyes, and pressed one of the buttons. When 49

I opened my eyes and looked out, I found myself in Ancient Egypt! I peered out the 66

window and saw warriors running towards me. They looked angry, so I pressed a 80

button that said "The Future" and quickly arrived back at my house. 92

I decided the time-travel machine was way cool and called my best friends, Jeff 107

and Justin. I didn't tell them about the time-travel machine over the phone because I 123

knew they wouldn't believe me. They always questioned the things I told them. 136

A few minutes later, I looked out my bedroom window. Sure enough, Jeff and 150

Justin were walking up the driveway. "Hey," I said. "You guys have to see the time 166

machine I found." 169

"You know we're too old for make-believe," Justin said as he folded his arms. 184

"No, I'm serious," I insisted, leading them to my machine. With their eyes wide 198

open, they stood in complete silence. After a lot of questions, they convinced me 212

they were ready to try it out. We crammed into the machine, and I randomly pressed 228

one of the buttons. Suddenly we found ourselves in medieval England. Jeff and 241

Justin were totally amazed. They couldn't believe their eyes! Just as we were about 255

to step out, we noticed several knights in shining armor approaching. I decided not 269

to chance it. I hit the future button, and we ended up safe and sound back in my 287

home. 288

Jeff and Justin made me promise to take them on another adventure very soon. 302

Hopefully, next time we will be able to stay longer and explore more of the past. 318

SCORE	_____	−	_____	=	_____
	words attempted in one minute		number of errors		words correct per minute (wcpm)

I wasn't very excited as my mother and I pulled into a parking lot filled with pot holes in front of a weather-beaten building. Through my smudged glasses, the building appeared very dull. Behind the building, I could see the ocean tossing and I wished my surprise was an ocean outing. I'd rather stroll along the seashore any day, than do whatever my mom planned to do in that dreary building. But before I could turn to complain to my mother, she'd already climbed out of the car.

"Great," I said, slamming the car door and taking my time as I followed her.

The building was about as spectacular on the inside as it was on the outside. There was a dumpy desk stacked with papers, a telephone ringing off the hook, and a row of empty chairs. I didn't see anything more interesting than a thick oak door and some dusty sailing equipment. There were piles of rope and rigging everywhere. Suddenly my mother was nowhere in sight. I couldn't imagine what kind of surprise this deserted office could produce. "I can see this is going to be an exciting day," I muttered to myself.

"Are you Jesse?" asked a voice. A young woman stood on the far end of the office. "Your mother asked me to make sure you could find your way. Everyone is already outside." Curiously, I followed the woman across the threadbare carpet to the rear of the building.

The woman yanked the door open, and we stepped out, blinking in the sunshine. Before me was the smell of the sea, a stretch of beach, and a gorgeous ship bobbing on the waves. My mom was already on board.

"What exactly was going on here?" I wondered to myself.

My mother must have felt me watching her, because she spun around and started waving her arms at me. She was beckoning me down the dangerous-looking dock toward the impressive ship.

"Surprise, Jesse!" she shouted. "Do you want to go whale watching with me? Captain Jones tells me that a pod of Humpback whales was just spotted feeding outside the bay. Hurry up, lazybones!"

I couldn't think of anything sarcastic to say to that. In fact, I was so excited that I skipped down the beach toward the boat. I guess my mom knew how to surprise me after all.

I wasn't very excited as my mother and I pulled into a parking lot filled with pot   17
holes in front of a weather-beaten building. Through my smudged glasses, the   30
building appeared very dull. Behind the building, I could see the ocean tossing and I   45
wished my surprise was an ocean outing. I'd rather stroll along the seashore any   59
day, than do whatever my mom planned to do in that dreary building. But before I   75
could turn to complain to my mother, she'd already climbed out of the car.   89

"Great," I said, slamming the car door and taking my time as I followed her.   104

The building was about as spectacular on the inside as it was on the outside.   119
There was a dumpy desk stacked with papers, a telephone ringing off the hook, and   134
a row of empty chairs. I didn't see anything more interesting than a thick oak door   150
and some dusty sailing equipment. There were piles of rope and rigging   162
everywhere. Suddenly my mother was nowhere in sight. I couldn't imagine what   174
kind of surprise this deserted office could produce. "I can see this is going to be an   191
exciting day," I muttered to myself.   197

"Are you Jesse?" asked a voice. A young woman stood on the far end of the   213
office. "Your mother asked me to make sure you could find your way. Everyone is   228
already outside." Curiously, I followed the woman across the threadbare carpet to   240
the rear of the building.   245

The woman yanked the door open, and we stepped out, blinking in the sunshine.   259
Before me was the smell of the sea, a stretch of beach, and a gorgeous ship   275
bobbing on the waves. My mom was already on board.   285

"What exactly was going on here?" I wondered to myself.   295

My mother must have felt me watching her, because she spun around and   308
started waving her arms at me. She was beckoning me down the dangerous-looking   322
dock toward the impressive ship.   327

"Surprise, Jesse!" she shouted. "Do you want to go whale watching with me?   340
Captain Jones tells me that a pod of Humpback whales was just spotted feeding   354
outside the bay. Hurry up, lazybones!"   360

I couldn't think of anything sarcastic to say to that. In fact, I was so excited that I 378
skipped down the beach toward the boat. I guess my mom knew how to surprise me   394
after all.   396

SCORE	_____	−	_____	=	_____
	words attempted in one minute		number of errors		words correct per minute (wcpm)

© Edformation, Inc.

I'm going to be an astronaut when I grow up. As soon as they accept me into NASA, I'm destined for distant planets and far off galaxies. I'll be the captain of a spaceship. That means I'll be the one in charge of blasting off and landing on Mars and all sorts of other spectacular stuff.

Billy Jones, a boy in my class, doesn't believe me. He calls me a liar and teases me all through recess. "Mary Kate is an alien!" he hollers from the monkey bars. All the kids hear him, and almost everyone laughs.

The only one who doesn't laugh is my best friend, Roger. That's because he's going to be an astronaut someday too. Roger wants to be the scientist aboard the space shuttle. He wants to bring white rats, microscopes, and all kinds of experiments up into space. That way, he can do tests and record his results as we orbit the planet Earth.

Of course, we'll run into aliens during our fantastic travels and adventures. I'll be such a highly trained and skilled space captain that they'll agree to have tea with us aboard our spaceship. I'll serve them ginger tea from my special tea pot and tempt them with delicate cookies made out of thin wafers, frosted with vanilla, and dipped in chocolate. Because the sun never sets in outer space, we'll laugh and talk for days. Then as we hover in the shadow of Earth, we'll say goodbye but promise to visit often.

At night before I snuggle into my bed, I go to the window and look out at the stars. I imagine what it's going to be like one day to float among them. When my mom comes into the bedroom and asks me what I'm thinking about, I tell her all about my dreams.

"You can do anything you set your mind to, Mary Kate," she says before she smiles and kisses me goodnight.

So, I don't care what Billy Jones shouts as he hangs upside down from the monkey bars, and I don't care who chuckles at my expense. I know I'm destined for great things. I know it right down to the tips of my toes.

I'm going to be an astronaut when I grow up. As soon as they accept me into   17

NASA, I'm destined for distant planets and far off galaxies. I'll be the captain of a   33

spaceship. That means I'll be the one in charge of blasting off and landing on Mars   49

and all sorts of other spectacular stuff.   56

Billy Jones, a boy in my class, doesn't believe me. He calls me a liar and teases   73

me all through recess. "Mary Kate is an alien!" he hollers from the monkey bars. All   89

the kids hear him, and almost everyone laughs.   97

The only one who doesn't laugh is my best friend, Roger. That's because he's   111

going to be an astronaut someday too. Roger wants to be the scientist aboard the   126

space shuttle. He wants to bring white rats, microscopes, and all kinds of   139

experiments up into space. That way, he can do tests and record his results as we   155

orbit the planet Earth.   159

Of course, we'll run into aliens during our fantastic travels and adventures. I'll be   173

such a highly trained and skilled space captain that they'll agree to have tea with us   189

aboard our spaceship. I'll serve them ginger tea from my special tea pot and tempt   204

them with delicate cookies made out of thin wafers, frosted with vanilla, and dipped   218

in chocolate. Because the sun never sets in outer space, we'll laugh and talk for   233

days. Then as we hover in the shadow of Earth, we'll say goodbye but promise to   249

visit often.   251

At night before I snuggle into my bed, I go to the window and look out at the   269

stars. I imagine what it's going to be like one day to float among them. When my   286

mom comes into the bedroom and asks me what I'm thinking about, I tell her all   302

about my dreams.   305

"You can do anything you set your mind to, Mary Kate," she says before she   320

smiles and kisses me goodnight.   325

So, I don't care what Billy Jones shouts as he hangs upside down from the   340

monkey bars, and I don't care who chuckles at my expense. I know I'm destined for   356

great things. I know it right down to the tips of my toes.   369

SCORE	_____	-	_____	=	_____
	words attempted in one minute		number of errors		words correct per minute (wcpm)

It was a cold and dreary day. A few leaves clung desperately to the branches of the solitary trees, but most of the leaves had been ripped off as the wind gusted through. It was only the middle of October, but already the wind was bitterly cold. Even the trees seemed to shiver.

One house stood alone, surrounded by barren fields. It seemed lonely and vulnerable. There were patches on the roof where the shingles had come off and most of the paint was chipping away. The house looked shabby and neglected.

The inside of the house was no cheerier. Its three rooms were starkly furnished, and the floor was bare except for a few ragged-looking rugs. The only point of interest in the living room was the large, crudely made easel that sat near the eastern window.

A slender, aging man stood before the easel in bedraggled clothes and bare feet. He was painting a beach on the canvas before him. It was a lovely scene depicting sand, water, and the vibrant colors of a sunset.

The man was pleased with his work thus far. He had awakened to the gloomy day, and his mood was as bleak as the weather outside. Breakfast had been a hurried affair because he was eager to get to work and dispel the aching sadness in his heart.

As soon as the man began to splash color on the canvas, his despair started to evaporate. He began to drift away, his concentration entirely on the emerging picture before him. His loneliness and hopelessness left him, like a heavy shawl lifted from his shoulders. It was as if he were a part of the scene before him, his memory and rendition of it more real than his dismal surroundings.

Then the man added the final element to the painting. It was a woman, lovely and graceful. She was approaching the painter, her arm lifted in salutation and a radiant smile on her face.

As the man completed the final touches of the painting he felt great joy. Painting could brighten even his darkest days.

It was a cold and dreary day. A few leaves clung desperately to the branches of	16
the solitary trees, but most of the leaves had been ripped off as the wind gusted	32
through. It was only the middle of October, but already the wind was bitterly cold.	47
Even the trees seemed to shiver.	53
One house stood alone, surrounded by barren fields. It seemed lonely and	65
vulnerable. There were patches on the roof where the shingles had come off and	79
most of the paint was chipping away. The house looked shabby and neglected.	92
The inside of the house was no cheerier. Its three rooms were starkly furnished,	106
and the floor was bare except for a few ragged-looking rugs. The only point of	122
interest in the living room was the large, crudely made easel that sat near the	137
eastern window.	139
A slender, aging man stood before the easel in bedraggled clothes and bare feet.	153
He was painting a beach on the canvas before him. It was a lovely scene depicting	169
sand, water, and the vibrant colors of a sunset.	178
The man was pleased with his work thus far. He had awakened to the gloomy	193
day, and his mood was as bleak as the weather outside. Breakfast had been a	208
hurried affair because he was eager to get to work and dispel the aching sadness in	224
his heart.	226
As soon as the man began to splash color on the canvas, his despair started to	242
evaporate. He began to drift away, his concentration entirely on the emerging	254
picture before him. His loneliness and hopelessness left him, like a heavy shawl	267
lifted from his shoulders. It was as if he were a part of the scene before him, his	285
memory and rendition of it more real than his dismal surroundings.	296
Then the man added the final element to the painting. It was a woman, lovely	311
and graceful. She was approaching the painter, her arm lifted in salutation and a	325
radiant smile on her face.	330
As the man completed the final touches of the painting he felt great joy. Painting	345
could brighten even his darkest days.	351

SCORE	_____	−	_____	=	_____
	words attempted in one minute		number of errors		words correct per minute (wcpm)

Late one afternoon, Patrick O'Connor was walking home from school when a strange thing happened. His usual route home took him through a dark tunnel and high along some cliffs near an ocean. He saw nothing in the tunnel that amazed him. He didn't see anything strange as he walked along the cliffs above the wild waters. But just as he turned down the lane that led to his grandmother's cottage, a strange sight caught his eye.

It was a fairy sitting cool as a cucumber on a corner fencepost. Patrick stopped, closed his eyes, rubbed them, and then opened them again. The fairy was still sitting on the fencepost, and now she was staring at him. The tiny, shimmering woman was the most beautiful creature Patrick had ever seen. She had long, glossy hair and wings like a butterfly.

"I've been waiting for you all afternoon, Patrick O'Connor," she said. "What took you so long to walk home from school?"

"I didn't know anyone was waiting for me, so I had no reason to hurry," Patrick stammered.

"That's an honest answer," she told Patrick. Then she stood up and flapped her pretty wings. Before Patrick realized what was happening, she'd already landed on his shoulder and propped her elbow on his ear.

"Patrick O'Connor," she whispered. "Did you know your grandmother was friends with the fairies in these parts?"

"No, I did not know that," Patrick replied. "What do you want with me?"

"Well, now that you and your family live in your grandmother's house, the fairies want to be your friends as well. I was the one chosen to speak with you. Has anyone ever told you that you have your grandmother's eyes?" Patrick blushed and shoved his hands in his pockets as the fairy smiled kindly at him.

"I must go now, but we will speak again very soon," the fairy said as she blew him a kiss and disappeared.

Late one afternoon, Patrick O'Connor was walking home from school when a   12

strange thing happened. His usual route home took him through a dark tunnel and   26

high along some cliffs near an ocean. He saw nothing in the tunnel that amazed   41

him. He didn't see anything strange as he walked along the cliffs above the wild   56

waters. But just as he turned down the lane that led to his grandmother's cottage, a   72

strange sight caught his eye.   77

It was a fairy sitting cool as a cucumber on a corner fencepost. Patrick stopped,   92

closed his eyes, rubbed them, and then opened them again. The fairy was still   106

sitting on the fencepost, and now she was staring at him. The tiny, shimmering   120

woman was the most beautiful creature Patrick had ever seen. She had long, glossy   134

hair and wings like a butterfly.   140

"I've been waiting for you all afternoon, Patrick O'Connor," she said. "What took   153

you so long to walk home from school?"   161

"I didn't know anyone was waiting for me, so I had no reason to hurry," Patrick   177

stammered.   178

"That's an honest answer," she told Patrick. Then she stood up and flapped her   192

pretty wings. Before Patrick realized what was happening, she'd already landed on   204

his shoulder and propped her elbow on his ear.   213

"Patrick O'Connor," she whispered. "Did you know your grandmother was friends   224

with the fairies in these parts?"   230

"No, I did not know that," Patrick replied. "What do you want with me?"   244

"Well, now that you and your family live in your grandmother's house, the fairies   258

want to be your friends as well. I was the one chosen to speak with you. Has   275

anyone ever told you that you have your grandmother's eyes?" Patrick blushed and   288

shoved his hands in his pockets as the fairy smiled kindly at him.   301

"I must go now, but we will speak again very soon," the fairy said as she blew   318

him a kiss and disappeared.   323

SCORE _____ – _____ = _____
| words attempted in one minute | number of errors | words correct per minute (wcpm) |

Laura was very excited that there were only three days of school this week. The long weekend was going to be great because Laura was going to stay with her grandma and grandpa. She always liked to stay with them because it was so much fun.

Mrs. Stevens gave a spelling test on Wednesday morning, but Laura could hardly think because she kept imagining what she was going to do after school. She needed to pack her clothes in her new black suitcase. She also needed to bring her favorite book because each night everyone would sit by the fireplace and read. Finally, she couldn't forget Mrs. Mouse, her favorite stuffed animal, who had slept next to her in bed since she was little.

By the afternoon, Laura had an even harder time listening to her teacher. Laura thought about other nights at her grandparents' house. She knew that she'd have to be in bed before 8:30, even if it wasn't a school night. She also remembered the rule to eat ALL your vegetables. Still, most of the differences were fun. Grandma would always let Laura rent a movie and eat popcorn on the couch. Better yet, Laura would be able to hear stories about things HER dad had done when he was a kid. Best of all, Grandma would ask her how she felt about different things, and Laura would always feel safe talking.

That night, when Laura's dad dropped her off at Grandma's, he surprised Laura by picking her up after he'd grabbed the black suitcase. He teased her by saying the suitcase was heavier than she was.

"Have a super weekend, Peanut," he said as he rang the doorbell. "I wish I didn't have to work out of town, but I do. Have a great time, and I'll see you Sunday night."

Grandma opened the front door and gave Laura a big hug. Grandpa took her suitcase and carried it upstairs pretending like it was heavy. Laura heard popcorn popping in the microwave. She looked at the coffee table and saw the movie she wanted to see about a girl's basketball team.

"Yes," thought Laura. "This weekend is going to be great!"

© Edformation, Inc.

Laura was very excited that there were only three days of school this week. The   15

long weekend was going to be great because Laura was going to stay with her   30

grandma and grandpa. She always liked to stay with them because it was so much   45

fun.   46

     Mrs. Stevens gave a spelling test on Wednesday morning, but Laura could hardly   59

think because she kept imagining what she was going to do after school. She   73

needed to pack her clothes in her new black suitcase. She also needed to bring her   89

favorite book because each night everyone would sit by the fireplace and read.   102

Finally, she couldn't forget Mrs. Mouse, her favorite stuffed animal, who had slept   115

next to her in bed since she was little.   124

     By the afternoon, Laura had an even harder time listening to her teacher. Laura   138

thought about other nights at her grandparents' house. She knew that she'd have to   152

be in bed before 8:30, even if it wasn't a school night. She also remembered the   168

rule to eat ALL your vegetables. Still, most of the differences were fun. Grandma   182

would always let Laura rent a movie and eat popcorn on the couch. Better yet,   197

Laura would be able to hear stories about things HER dad had done when he was a   214

kid. Best of all, Grandma would ask her how she felt about different things, and   229

Laura would always feel safe talking.   235

     That night, when Laura's dad dropped her off at Grandma's, he surprised Laura   248

by picking her up after he'd grabbed the black suitcase. He teased her by saying the   264

suitcase was heavier than she was.   270

     "Have a super weekend, Peanut," he said as he rang the doorbell. "I wish I didn't   286

have to work out of town, but I do. Have a great time, and I'll see you Sunday night."   305

     Grandma opened the front door and gave Laura a big hug. Grandpa took her   319

suitcase and carried it upstairs pretending like it was heavy. Laura heard popcorn   332

popping in the microwave. She looked at the coffee table and saw the movie she   347

wanted to see about a girl's basketball team.   355

     "Yes," thought Laura. "This weekend is going to be great!"   365

SCORE	_____	−	_____	=	_____
	words attempted in one minute		number of errors		words correct per minute (wcpm)

© Edformation, Inc.

"Let's go exploring," suggested Amanda. "I've always dreamed of discovering treasures left behind by pioneers."

"Weren't many pioneers rather poor?" Beth asked thoughtfully. "I never thought of pioneers leaving behind treasures. It may be possible that because their wagons couldn't carry everything, travelers buried their belongings and hoped they could return for them later."

"I don't care who left it or why. I just want to find someone's long lost money, jewels, gold, or silver! Don't you ever daydream about becoming rich overnight?"

"Not really," replied Beth. "If I found a lot of money, I'd probably just spend it foolishly and it would be gone before I knew it."

"What if you found gold or jewels?" asked Amanda. "Wouldn't it be fun to wear bangles or hair pieces that were once owned by queens or princesses?"

"Even though I only wear blue jeans and T-shirts, I suppose it would be amusing to decorate my ears and long hair with jewels," laughed Beth. "You know I detest dresses, and I usually wear a ponytail. I doubt very much that jewels would go with my wardrobe!"

"Does that mean you want to stay home and play something else?" asked Amanda.

"No way," cried Beth. "Let's go exploring! You never know what we'll find. We may discover the long lost treasure you've been dreaming of, or we could find some old books or a long-lost letter. Even if we don't find anything, the search will be fun. We can start at my grandma's place down by the river. Let's telephone her to get her permission. Maybe we'll get really lucky, and she will bake cookies for us!"

After the girls got to Beth's grandma's house and finished their cookies and milk, they ran off towards the river. Oh my, what a dilemma. Where should they start looking? Since centuries had passed and no trails remained, the pioneers could have buried their belongings almost anywhere.

The girls sat on the riverbank and pretended they were early pioneers traveling through the area. What would it feel like to leave behind things you love, knowing you might never return? As they imagined life as pioneers, the sun set. Eventually they ran back to the house to have dinner and ask Beth's grandma what she knew about the pioneers.

"Let's go exploring," suggested Amanda. "I've always dreamed of discovering   10

treasures left behind by pioneers."   15

"Weren't many pioneers rather poor?" Beth asked thoughtfully. "I never thought   26

of pioneers leaving behind treasures. It may be possible that because their wagons   39

couldn't carry everything, travelers buried their belongings and hoped they could   50

return for them later."   54

"I don't care who left it or why. I just want to find someone's long lost money,   71

jewels, gold, or silver! Don't you ever daydream about becoming rich overnight?"   83

"Not really," replied Beth. "If I found a lot of money, I'd probably just spend it   99

foolishly and it would be gone before I knew it."   109

"What if you found gold or jewels?" asked Amanda. "Wouldn't it be fun to wear   124

bangles or hair pieces that were once owned by queens or princesses?"   136

"Even though I only wear blue jeans and T-shirts, I suppose it would be amusing   151

to decorate my ears and long hair with jewels," laughed Beth. "You know I detest   166

dresses, and I usually wear a ponytail. I doubt very much that jewels would go with   182

my wardrobe!"   184

"Does that mean you want to stay home and play something else?" asked   197

Amanda.   198

"No way," cried Beth. "Let's go exploring! You never know what we'll find. We   212

may discover the long lost treasure you've been dreaming of, or we could find some   227

old books or a long-lost letter. Even if we don't find anything, the search will be fun.   245

We can start at my grandma's place down by the river. Let's telephone her to get   261

her permission. Maybe we'll get really lucky, and she will bake cookies for us!"   275

After the girls got to Beth's grandma's house and finished their cookies and milk,   289

they ran off towards the river. Oh my, what a dilemma. Where should they start   304

looking? Since centuries had passed and no trails remained, the pioneers could   316

have buried their belongings almost anywhere.   322

The girls sat on the riverbank and pretended they were early pioneers traveling   335

through the area. What would it feel like to leave behind things you love, knowing   350

you might never return? As they imagined life as pioneers, the sun set. Eventually   364

they ran back to the house to have dinner and ask Beth's grandma what she knew   380

about the pioneers.   383

SCORE	_____	−	_____	=	_____
	words attempted in one minute		number of errors		words correct per minute (wcpm)

Little Wolf's mother was hungry for rabbit stew one morning, so she told her son to go out and shoot a rabbit for her. She said she would make a savory stew for dinner. Little Wolf was happy because he loved to hunt. He was good with a bow and arrow and rarely missed when he shot at an animal.

Little Wolf wasn't in the forest for very long before he came upon a rabbit and took aim. He was just about to release his arrow when the rabbit turned and spoke to him.

"Oh, please don't shoot me, brave hunter," the rabbit pleaded. "I am the mother of five defenseless babies. If you kill me, my children will starve."

Little Wolf did not lower his bow and continued to aim the arrow right between the rabbit's pleading eyes.

"My mother is hungry for rabbit stew," he told her. "She sent me out into the forest for rabbit and will be very angry if I return with nothing."

"Return with nothing, wise hunter. If you let me go so I may tend to my babies, I will give you the best of luck with my magical powers."

"Bah!" Little Wolf said. "We do not need luck. We need food." Still, even though Little Wolf was famished, he could not shoot the rabbit because she had spoken to him.

"Go on then. I will shoot another rabbit," he said. Despite the good luck promised to him, he returned that evening without a rabbit for his mother's stew.

"You lazy boy!" his mother shouted at him. "Go down to the river and fetch some water for me."

On the trail to the river, Little Wolf thought he caught a glimpse of the rabbit he'd let go earlier, but it was too dark to be certain. When he got to the river, he dipped his mother's jug into the current, only to pull it out and find a silver trout trapped inside. Little Wolf tossed the trout on the beach, dipped the jug again, and out came another fish!

"What luck!" Little Wolf said. He and his mother had savory trout stew for dinner. Little Wolf thought trout stew was better than rabbit stew any day.

Little Wolf's mother was hungry for rabbit stew one morning, so she told her son   15

to go out and shoot a rabbit for her. She said she would make a savory stew for   33

dinner. Little Wolf was happy because he loved to hunt. He was good with a bow   49

and arrow and rarely missed when he shot at an animal.   60

Little Wolf wasn't in the forest for very long before he came upon a rabbit and   76

took aim. He was just about to release his arrow when the rabbit turned and spoke   92

to him.   94

"Oh, please don't shoot me, brave hunter," the rabbit pleaded. "I am the mother   108

of five defenseless babies. If you kill me, my children will starve."   120

Little Wolf did not lower his bow and continued to aim the arrow right between the   136

rabbit's pleading eyes.   139

"My mother is hungry for rabbit stew," he told her. "She sent me out into the   155

forest for rabbit and will be very angry if I return with nothing."   168

"Return with nothing, wise hunter. If you let me go so I may tend to my babies, I   186

will give you the best of luck with my magical powers."   197

"Bah!" Little Wolf said. "We do not need luck. We need food." Still, even though   212

Little Wolf was famished, he could not shoot the rabbit because she had spoken to   227

him.   228

"Go on then. I will shoot another rabbit," he said. Despite the good luck   242

promised to him, he returned that evening without a rabbit for his mother's stew.   256

"You lazy boy!" his mother shouted at him. "Go down to the river and fetch some   272

water for me."   275

On the trail to the river, Little Wolf thought he caught a glimpse of the rabbit he'd   292

let go earlier, but it was too dark to be certain. When he got to the river, he dipped   311

his mother's jug into the current, only to pull it out and find a silver trout trapped   328

inside. Little Wolf tossed the trout on the beach, dipped the jug again, and out came   344

another fish!   346

"What luck!" Little Wolf said. He and his mother had savory trout stew for dinner.   361

Little Wolf thought trout stew was better than rabbit stew any day.   373

SCORE	_____ words attempted in one minute	−	_____ number of errors	=	_____ words correct per minute (wcpm)

Molly tried to sleep, but she couldn't. Every time she closed her eyes and tried to snuggle her pillows, she would remember that tomorrow it would be her turn to stand up in front of the class, in front of EVERYONE, and give her speech.

Molly couldn't help it, she was nervous. Tonight when her mom tucked her into bed, she folded the covers around Molly more snugly than usual.

"I know you're nervous because of your speech tomorrow, Molly, but you really have nothing to be scared of."

Molly couldn't speak, so she nodded instead. Her mom didn't really know what Molly was so nervous about. Her mom was thirty-five years old, not eight years old and in fourth grade like Molly.

She didn't know that Michael O'Connor sat in the front row of Molly's class. She didn't know that whenever a girl got up to give her speech, he made funny faces and stuck his tongue out at her.

What if Molly stood in front of the class tomorrow and found she couldn't speak? What if she blushed until she was as red as a beet? What if her eyes popped out and rolled between the aisles to the teacher's desk? What if everyone laughed at her?

Molly's speech was about the lions in Africa. It was about how they lived in families called "prides" and how lionesses did all the hunting. What if nobody cared about lions?

Molly didn't remember falling asleep. She must have slept because the next time she opened her eyes it was morning and time to go to school. Even though she was more than a little bit scared and so nervous she could only eat half her cereal, she still went.

When it was time for Molly to give her speech, the whole classroom suddenly got quiet. Molly went to the front of the room, her hands trembling. There was Michael O'Connor crossing his eyes. Molly looked at him and then looked away.

"Lions live in Africa," Molly said and went on with her speech.

Mr. Shrunk worked as a filing clerk at the telephone company. All day long he   15

filed names, names, and more names. Mr. Shrunk thought his job was probably the   29

most boring job on the planet.   35

One day, Mr. Shrunk could not take it any longer. Even though he was in the   51

middle of organizing a huge stack of folders, he stood up, put on his jacket, and   67

walked out the door.   71

"That's the last I'll ever see of that place," he said to himself as he climbed into   88

his car and drove home. "Now I need to find myself a new and more exciting job."   105

The next morning over a bowl of chocolate crunch cereal, Mr. Shrunk reviewed   118

the classifieds in the daily paper.   124

"It looks like they need help at both the police station and the fire station. I'll   140

apply at both places," he said to himself. Mr. Shrunk finished his cereal, changed   154

out of his pajamas and slippers into a suit and tie, and went out to look for work.   172

First, he stopped at the police station, where he got the chance to ride around   187

with a pair of police officers in their squad car. An hour later, Mr. Shrunk decided   203

dodging bullets and high-speed chases were not for him.   213

At the fire station, the firemen asked Mr. Shrunk to climb five stories of ladders   228

and then slide down the long fire pole. Since he was afraid of heights and burning   244

objects, he left the fire station without a job.   253

The next morning, Mr. Shrunk reviewed the classified ads yet again. He was   266

about to set aside the paper when an ad on the far corner of the page caught his   284

attention.   285

The ad read, "Brave stunt man wanted for dangerous stunts in a feature   298

Hollywood film." The ad said the studio was looking for a tall man with a medium   314

build and a mustache. The ad also gave the number to call if interested. Mr. Shrunk   330

stood up.   332

"I'm tall," he said. "I have a medium build and a mustache." He marched across   347

his kitchen and picked up the telephone. Mr. Shrunk was sure tomorrow he would   361

start a new job.   365

SCORE   _____ − _____ = _____
words attempted   number of errors   words correct per
in one minute   minute (wcpm)

My name is Elmer, and I'm nearly six years old. Six years old is about 42 dog years, so it is a little embarrassing to tell you that I got lost at my age. Actually, I got lost because I listened to my kennel mate, Abby, who often gets us into trouble.

We traveled from Illinois to Michigan to see our owners' relatives. It was a long ride, and our owners did quite a bit of visiting when they arrived. I guess that's why we missed our long daily walk. When they let us out the next morning, Abby took advantage of the situation and started running. I impulsively followed her!

We were exploring a new neighborhood, and the next thing I knew, two black Labradors appeared and started sniffing me all over. Abby bolted towards the highway and left me to fend for myself. The labs' owner, who seemed mean at that moment, tried to control her noisy dogs. Finally, she placed her hands on her hips and firmly yelled, "Kennel!" I understood that word, so I ran into the kennel with the labs. I guess I wasn't supposed to go inside because she dragged me out by my collar.

The lady commanded me to sit. She read my tags and giggled. Then she asked a familiar but embarrassing question. "Elmer? What kind of name is that for a handsome dog like yourself?" She called my owners' number and left a message for them. My owners quickly returned her call and made arrangements to pick me up. She fed me some biscuits and called her office to say she'd be late. She offered me a portable kennel to sit in while my owners came to get me. My owners were happy to see me. They thanked the nice lady before she left for work.

Some people say it's a dog eat dog world out there, but I disagree. Especially when you are lucky enough to get lost near a kind dog owner. However, I know I was lucky, and I think I've learned my lesson. The next time Abby wants to go exploring, I'll remind her that there's no place like home.

My name is Elmer, and I'm nearly six years old. Six years old is about 42 dog   17

years, so it is a little embarrassing to tell you that I got lost at my age. Actually, I got   37

lost because I listened to my kennel mate, Abby, who often gets us into trouble.   52

We traveled from Illinois to Michigan to see our owners' relatives. It was a long   67

ride, and our owners did quite a bit of visiting when they arrived. I guess that's why   84

we missed our long daily walk. When they let us out the next morning, Abby took   100

advantage of the situation and started running. I impulsively followed her!   111

We were exploring a new neighborhood, and the next thing I knew, two black   125

Labradors appeared and started sniffing me all over. Abby bolted towards the   137

highway and left me to fend for myself. The labs' owner, who seemed mean at that   153

moment, tried to control her noisy dogs. Finally, she placed her hands on her hips   168

and firmly yelled, "Kennel!" I understood that word, so I ran into the kennel with the   184

labs. I guess I wasn't supposed to go inside because she dragged me out by my   200

collar.   201

The lady commanded me to sit. She read my tags and giggled. Then she asked   216

a familiar but embarrassing question. "Elmer? What kind of name is that for a   230

handsome dog like yourself?" She called my owners' number and left a message for   243

them. My owners quickly returned her call and made arrangements to pick me up.   257

She fed me some biscuits and called her office to say she'd be late. She offered me   273

a portable kennel to sit in while my owners came to get me. My owners were happy   290

to see me. They thanked the nice lady before she left for work.   305

Some people say it's a dog eat dog world out there, but I disagree. Especially   320

when you are lucky enough to get lost near a kind dog owner. However, I know I was   338

lucky, and I think I've learned my lesson. The next time Abby wants to go exploring,   354

I'll remind her that there's no place like home.   363

SCORE _____ — _____ = _____
words attempted   number of errors   words correct per
in one minute   minute (wcpm)

Old Mr. Jenkins was digging around in his flower garden one afternoon when his hoe hit something solid. He put down the hoe and picked up a shovel.

"It must be one of those pesky rocks again," he told his cat, Virginia, who was always watching him. "When will I get rid of all of the rocks in my garden? I've been digging up rocks for more than fifty years."

"Meow," Virginia said as she watched Mr. Jenkins turn and start digging.

The rock that Mr. Jenkins hit with his hoe was long and narrow. It was soft, brown in color, and had two rounded ends. At first Mr. Jenkins thought he was digging up a petrified log. Soon though, he realized he was digging up a fossilized bone.

"Good heavens!" Mr. Jenkins exclaimed when he'd finally unearthed the bone and saw how huge it was. "What do you make of this thing, Virginia?"

Virginia, the cat, leaped gracefully down into the hole Mr. Jenkins just dug.

Mr. Jenkins could tell Virginia was thinking as she paced the length of the bone. Finally, Virginia stopped. She jumped out of the hole and stopped five feet across the lawn from it. She began to dig another hole with her furry paws.

Mr. Jenkins was about to scold Virginia because she was digging in the middle of his tulip patch, but he was curious. Instead of hollering, he picked up his shovel and went to help.

An hour later, Virginia and Mr. Jenkins dug up another bone. This bone was the skull of a dinosaur. It was as big as Mr. Jenkins' lawn mower and had rows and rows of sharp teeth. The teeth were the same size as the blade on Mr. Jenkins' hoe. When Mr. Jenkins saw the skull, he set it down carefully and walked into his house. From his kitchen, he used the telephone and called the local museum.

"I've got something out in my garden I think you'll want to see," he told the scientist who answered the phone. "Bring shovels!"

Old Mr. Jenkins was digging around in his flower garden one afternoon when his	14
hoe hit something solid. He put down the hoe and picked up a shovel.	28
"It must be one of those pesky rocks again," he told his cat, Virginia, who was	44
always watching him. "When will I get rid of all of the rocks in my garden? I've been	62
digging up rocks for more than fifty years."	70
"Meow," Virginia said as she watched Mr. Jenkins turn and start digging.	82
The rock that Mr. Jenkins hit with his hoe was long and narrow. It was soft,	98
brown in color, and had two rounded ends. At first Mr. Jenkins thought he was	113
digging up a petrified log. Soon though, he realized he was digging up a fossilized	128
bone.	129
"Good heavens!" Mr. Jenkins exclaimed when he'd finally unearthed the bone	140
and saw how huge it was. "What do you make of this thing, Virginia?"	154
Virginia, the cat, leaped gracefully down into the hole Mr. Jenkins just dug.	167
Mr. Jenkins could tell Virginia was thinking as she paced the length of the bone.	182
Finally, Virginia stopped. She jumped out of the hole and stopped five feet across	196
the lawn from it. She began to dig another hole with her furry paws.	210
Mr. Jenkins was about to scold Virginia because she was digging in the middle of	225
his tulip patch, but he was curious. Instead of hollering, he picked up his shovel and	241
went to help.	244
An hour later, Virginia and Mr. Jenkins dug up another bone. This bone was the	259
skull of a dinosaur. It was as big as Mr. Jenkins' lawn mower and had rows and	276
rows of sharp teeth. The teeth were the same size as the blade on Mr. Jenkins' hoe.	293
When Mr. Jenkins saw the skull, he set it down carefully and walked into his house.	309
From his kitchen, he used the telephone and called the local museum.	321
"I've got something out in my garden I think you'll want to see," he told the	337
scientist who answered the phone. "Bring shovels!"	344

SCORE	_____ − _____ = _____
	words attempted number of errors words correct per
	in one minute minute (wcpm)

Once upon a time, in a small village called Bandion, there lived a boy called Samir. Samir had three roosters, and every morning they would say, "Cock-a-doodle-do! Cock-a-doodle-do!" As soon as Grandma heard their call, she would get up and start her day. They would call again, and Grandpa would rise and begin his day. When they called for the third time, Samir and his father, mother, and brothers would wake up and get ready for the new day. Everyone in Samir's family depended on the roosters to wake them up in the morning. Samir loved his roosters very much and took excellent care of them.

One day, two of Samir's uncles came to the village to visit. They stayed for several days. The roosters would say, "Cock-a-doodle-do" promptly at the stroke of every hour. Samir's uncles were impressed that his family didn't need a clock, and they wished they each had one of Samir's roosters. On the last day of their visit, Samir's uncles convinced him to give them each a rooster. After all, he did have three roosters and one rooster should be enough. Each uncle picked a rooster and left for their home.

Samir stroked the rooster that was left behind. "You are all alone now," he said sadly.

The next morning, the lone rooster did not crow. Grandma waited and waited for it to call. When Grandpa finally got up and left for work, he was late. Everyone in the family got up late that day, and everyone was angry.

"Why didn't the rooster crow?" everyone asked. Samir understood. The remaining rooster was lonely and missed his friends very much. Samir decided to write to his uncles and beg them to return their roosters. Before he could finish his letters, there was a knock at the door. Both of his uncles had returned with their roosters.

"Take your roosters back," they said. They did not crow this morning, and we were all late!"

Samir gathered his roosters into his arms and said, "You clever roosters. You planned not to crow if you were ever separated."

Once upon a time, in a small village called Bandion, there lived a boy called	15
Samir. Samir had three roosters, and every morning they would say, "Cock-a-	28
doodle-do! Cock-a-doodle-do!" As soon as Grandma heard their call, she would get	44
up and start her day. They would call again, and Grandpa would rise and begin his	60
day. When they called for the third time, Samir and his father, mother, and brothers	75
would wake up and get ready for the new day. Everyone in Samir's family depended	90
on the roosters to wake them up in the morning. Samir loved his roosters very much	106
and took excellent care of them.	112
One day, two of Samir's uncles came to the village to visit. They stayed for	127
several days. The roosters would say, "Cock-a-doodle-do" promptly at the stroke of	142
every hour. Samir's uncles were impressed that his family didn't need a clock, and	156
they wished they each had one of Samir's roosters. On the last day of their visit,	172
Samir's uncles convinced him to give them each a rooster. After all, he did have	187
three roosters and one rooster should be enough. Each uncle picked a rooster and	201
left for their home.	205
Samir stroked the rooster that was left behind. "You are all alone now," he said	220
sadly.	221
The next morning, the lone rooster did not crow. Grandma waited and waited for	235
it to call. When Grandpa finally got up and left for work, he was late. Everyone in	252
the family got up late that day, and everyone was angry.	263
"Why didn't the rooster crow?" everyone asked. Samir understood. The	273
remaining rooster was lonely and missed his friends very much. Samir decided to	286
write to his uncles and beg them to return their roosters. Before he could finish his	302
letters, there was a knock at the door. Both of his uncles had returned with their	318
roosters.	319
"Take your roosters back," they said. They did not crow this morning, and we	333
were all late!"	336
Samir gathered his roosters into his arms and said, "You clever roosters. You	349
planned not to crow if you were ever separated."	358

SCORE	_____ − _____ = _____
	words attempted in one minute number of errors words correct per minute (wcpm)

One day Addie was collecting seashells in the surf when the flash of a fish tail caught her eye. At first Addie thought she'd seen the tail of a really small whale, so she backed away. Suddenly, a woman's head popped up out of the water, and Addie saw that the tail belonged to a mermaid.

The mermaid had tangled green hair. She had webbed skin between her blue fingers and gills behind her ears. The scales on her tail were silver and green.

Addie was so surprised she dropped her seashells. Her mother had always told her that mermaids didn't exist.

"Do not be frightened of me," the mermaid said. "I'm the last of my kind living in these waters, and I'm terribly lonely. Would you like to come under the water with me? I'll give you a tour of the ocean."

Addie knew that she probably shouldn't go with the mermaid, but her curiosity was too fierce. Soon she found herself chin deep in the sea with the mermaid splashing beside her.

"I don't think I should go under the water," Addie said. "I don't have gills behind my ears like you do."

"Just hold my hand tightly, and everything will be all right," the mermaid replied. Then she took Addie's hand and dove under the water.

At first Addie panicked as the green waves swirled around her. But she quickly realized the mermaid was telling the truth. As long as Addie held onto her hand, she could breathe under water and swim like a fish.

"Come on now," the mermaid told Addie. Her voice sounded eerie under the water.

The mermaid gave Addie a tour of the coral reef, and they swam with a colony of harmless jellyfish. They even rode on the back of a giant sea turtle. When Addie finally let go of the mermaid's hand and waded out of the water, the sun was setting and she could hear her mother calling for her.

"Thanks," Addie said.

"Any time, friend," the mermaid replied, and with a flash of her tail, she was gone.

One day Addie was collecting seashells in the surf when the flash of a fish tail   16
caught her eye. At first Addie thought she'd seen the tail of a really small whale, so   33
she backed away. Suddenly, a woman's head popped up out of the water, and   47
Addie saw that the tail belonged to a mermaid.   56

The mermaid had tangled green hair. She had webbed skin between her blue   69
fingers and gills behind her ears. The scales on her tail were silver and green.   84

Addie was so surprised she dropped her seashells. Her mother had always told   97
her that mermaids didn't exist.   102

"Do not be frightened of me," the mermaid said. "I'm the last of my kind living in   119
these waters, and I'm terribly lonely. Would you like to come under the water with   134
me? I'll give you a tour of the ocean."   143

Addie knew that she probably shouldn't go with the mermaid, but her curiosity   156
was too fierce. Soon she found herself chin deep in the sea with the mermaid   171
splashing beside her.   174

"I don't think I should go under the water," Addie said. "I don't have gills behind   190
my ears like you do."   195

"Just hold my hand tightly, and everything will be all right," the mermaid replied.   209
Then she took Addie's hand and dove under the water.   219

At first Addie panicked as the green waves swirled around her. But she quickly   233
realized the mermaid was telling the truth. As long as Addie held onto her hand, she   249
could breathe under water and swim like a fish.   258

"Come on now," the mermaid told Addie. Her voice sounded eerie under the   271
water.   272

The mermaid gave Addie a tour of the coral reef, and they swam with a colony of   289
harmless jellyfish. They even rode on the back of a giant sea turtle. When Addie   304
finally let go of the mermaid's hand and waded out of the water, the sun was setting   321
and she could hear her mother calling for her.   330

"Thanks," Addie said.   333

"Any time, friend," the mermaid replied, and with a flash of her tail, she was gone.   349

SCORE	_____	−	_____	=	_____
	words attempted in one minute		number of errors		words correct per minute (wcpm)

One rainy afternoon, Roger found himself at his grandparents' house with nothing to do. The TV wouldn't work because of the thunderstorm booming outside, so Roger sat in a window seat, slumped over, staring out at the wet lawn and street.

Roger knew his grandma was in the kitchen preparing dinner, but he didn't want to husk corn, so he didn't go in there. He knew his grandpa was upstairs in his study, and since he could think of nothing better to do, he climbed the stairs and knocked on the study door.

"Come in," said Roger's grandpa. "Ah, Roger," he said when he saw his grandson. "I thought you were going to be your grandma coming to ask me to husk corn."

"That's why I'm not down in the kitchen," Roger said with a smile as he approached his grandpa's massive desk. "I hate husking corn, so I thought I'd see what you were doing, Grandpa."

There were tiny slips of paper spread out all over the desk. Each slip of paper bore a miniature picture, and Roger knew right away they were his grandpa's stamps. His grandpa had collected stamps for a very long time. Roger's grandpa saw him looking at the stamps and smiled.

"I was just looking at my stamps," he said. "Would you like to look at them? Some of them are magic, you know."

"No, I didn't know," Roger said.

"Sure they are," said Roger's grandpa. "All you have to do to get the magic to work is pick up a stamp, lick the back, and stick it to your forehead. The magic in the stamp will make you invisible." The old man's eyes twinkled. "You want to give it a try?" he asked.

Roger nodded his head yes, and then both he and his grandpa selected a stamp, licked it, and stuck it to their foreheads. Roger closed his eyes and opened them, but he was slightly disappointed when he could still see his grandpa.

"I can see you, and you can see me," his grandpa whispered, "but nobody else can see us."

The magic worked when Roger and his grandpa tiptoed down to the kitchen. Roger's grandma never even saw them or asked them to husk corn.

One rainy afternoon, Roger found himself at his grandparents' house with nothing   12

to do. The TV wouldn't work because of the thunderstorm booming outside, so   25

Roger sat in a window seat, slumped over, staring out at the wet lawn and street.   41

Roger knew his grandma was in the kitchen preparing dinner, but he didn't want   55

to husk corn, so he didn't go in there. He knew his grandpa was upstairs in his   72

study, and since he could think of nothing better to do, he climbed the stairs and   88

knocked on the study door.   93

"Come in," said Roger's grandpa. "Ah, Roger," he said when he saw his   106

grandson. "I thought you were going to be your grandma coming to ask me to husk   122

corn."   123

"That's why I'm not down in the kitchen," Roger said with a smile as he   138

approached his grandpa's massive desk. "I hate husking corn, so I thought I'd see   152

what you were doing, Grandpa."   157

There were tiny slips of paper spread out all over the desk. Each slip of paper   173

bore a miniature picture, and Roger knew right away they were his grandpa's   186

stamps. His grandpa had collected stamps for a very long time. Roger's grandpa   199

saw him looking at the stamps and smiled.   207

"I was just looking at my stamps," he said. "Would you like to look at them?   223

Some of them are magic, you know."   230

"No, I didn't know," Roger said.   236

"Sure they are," said Roger's grandpa. "All you have to do to get the magic to   252

work is pick up a stamp, lick the back, and stick it to your forehead. The magic in   270

the stamp will make you invisible." The old man's eyes twinkled. "You want to give   285

it a try?" he asked.   290

Roger nodded his head yes, and then both he and his grandpa selected a stamp,   305

licked it, and stuck it to their foreheads. Roger closed his eyes and opened them,   320

but he was slightly disappointed when he could still see his grandpa.   332

"I can see you, and you can see me," his grandpa whispered, "but nobody else   347

can see us."   350

The magic worked when Roger and his grandpa tiptoed down to the kitchen.   363

Roger's grandma never even saw them or asked them to husk corn.   375

SCORE   _____ − _____ = _____
  words attempted   number of errors   words correct per
  in one minute   minute (wcpm)

Randy was a raccoon, and he loved to act on stage. He was preparing an animal talent show. Randy scurried throughout the forest talking to the animals of the woods. He wanted each animal to perform one act in the animal talent show.

Soon the big night came. All the animals of the forest showed up for the performance. Randy organized the performers, and the first one to perform was Gretchen the goose.

Gretchen walked out on stage and said, "Thank you all for coming tonight. I've prepared a special song I would like to sing for you." She took a deep breath and honked. She honked and honked and honked. It did not sound very good, but it was the best that Gretchen could do. She bowed when she was finished, and all the animals clapped politely.

"Borris, you're next," said Randy. Borris the bear shyly walked out on stage staring at the floor.

"Uh, I am going to dance," said Borris. The bear danced a little, shuffling his feet back and forth. He soon forgot his shyness and began to really enjoy himself. He stood on his back feet and danced backwards and forwards. He turned around in a circle. He jumped from one foot to the other. The animals cheered and whistled. Borris's dance was really quite good.

Sue the songbird was up next. She sang a beautiful solo. Her performance was perfect, thanks to all her years of practicing. The animals sat in awed silence until she finished.

Robert the rabbit performed a play in which he acted as if a man was hunting him. First he ran away, then he ran back, and then he acted as if he were hit by a bullet. The animals clapped, but they were too scared by the drama to enjoy it.

Randy the raccoon was the last one to perform. He performed a wonderful drama about a king who was looking for a queen. The audience laughed and cried. The animals loved Randy's performance. They clapped and requested another performance.

"Please come to the next animal talent show, and you will see more," said Randy. All the animals of the forest left the talent show looking forward to the next performance.

Randy was a raccoon, and he loved to act on stage. He was preparing an   15
animal talent show. Randy scurried throughout the forest talking to the animals of   28
the woods. He wanted each animal to perform one act in the animal talent show.   43

Soon the big night came. All the animals of the forest showed up for the   58
performance. Randy organized the performers, and the first one to perform was   70
Gretchen the goose.   73

Gretchen walked out on stage and said, "Thank you all for coming tonight. I've   87
prepared a special song I would like to sing for you." She took a deep breath and   104
honked. She honked and honked and honked. It did not sound very good, but it   119
was the best that Gretchen could do. She bowed when she was finished, and all   134
the animals clapped politely.   138

"Borris, you're next," said Randy. Borris the bear shyly walked out on stage   151
staring at the floor.   155

"Uh, I am going to dance," said Borris. The bear danced a little, shuffling his feet   171
back and forth. He soon forgot his shyness and began to really enjoy himself. He   186
stood on his back feet and danced backwards and forwards. He turned around in a   201
circle. He jumped from one foot to the other. The animals cheered and whistled.   215
Borris's dance was really quite good.   221

Sue the songbird was up next. She sang a beautiful solo. Her performance was   235
perfect, thanks to all her years of practicing. The animals sat in awed silence until   250
she finished.   252

Robert the rabbit performed a play in which he acted as if a man was hunting   268
him. First he ran away, then he ran back, and then he acted as if he were hit by a   288
bullet. The animals clapped, but they were too scared by the drama to enjoy it.   303

Randy the raccoon was the last one to perform. He performed a wonderful   316
drama about a king who was looking for a queen. The audience laughed and cried.   331
The animals loved Randy's performance. They clapped and requested another   341
performance.   342

"Please come to the next animal talent show, and you will see more," said   356
Randy. All the animals of the forest left the talent show looking forward to the next   372
performance.   373

SCORE	_____ words attempted in one minute	−	_____ number of errors	=	_____ words correct per minute (wcpm)

Tad didn't pay much attention to the goldfish in the crystal bowl on his dresser. Most mornings he just tapped a bit of food into the bowl and went to school. He never talked to his pet. He never admired the fish's golden scales or delicate fins and tail, and he didn't notice the skillful way in which the fish swam circles in the water.

One day Tad was feeding his fish and thinking about the monster movie he planned to see that evening, when the fish spoke to him.

"Hey," the fish gargled, "you're dumping too much food into my bowl. Watch what you're doing, foolish boy!" Tad was so surprised he dropped the container of fish food on the floor.

"No," he said to himself as he shook his head. "It isn't possible for my fish to speak to me because fish don't talk. This kind of thing only happens in monster movies, not in reality."

"This is happening to you," the fish proclaimed. "I'm a goldfish, and I'm speaking to you, young man. You've ignored me since the day you got me. For one thing, the water in this bowl is too cold. Just dip your finger in it, and test it yourself. I don't know how I've survived under these cruel conditions."

Of course, the water in the bowl wasn't too cold for the goldfish, but how was Tad to know? How was Tad to know that his goldfish was not an ordinary fish, and as soon as he dipped his finger into the water, he would trade places with the goldfish?

Tad stuck his finger in the water and found it was cold, but not freezing. "It feels just fine to me," he tried to say, but no sound escaped him. Tad was now trapped in the fish bowl, and the goldfish had become a little boy. Tad swam around the fish bowl frantically, but when he tried to speak, only bubbles came out of his mouth. He watched his fish, who was now a boy, move around his bedroom.

"I think I'll try to see one of those monster movies you mentioned," he told Tad. "Goodbye, Tadpole."

Tad didn't pay much attention to the goldfish in the crystal bowl on his dresser. 15

Most mornings he just tapped a bit of food into the bowl and went to school. He 32

never talked to his pet. He never admired the fish's golden scales or delicate fins 47

and tail, and he didn't notice the skillful way in which the fish swam circles in the 64

water. 65

One day Tad was feeding his fish and thinking about the monster movie he 79

planned to see that evening, when the fish spoke to him. 90

"Hey," the fish gargled, "you're dumping too much food into my bowl. Watch 103

what you're doing, foolish boy!" Tad was so surprised he dropped the container of 117

fish food on the floor. 122

"No," he said to himself as he shook his head. "It isn't possible for my fish to 139

speak to me because fish don't talk. This kind of thing only happens in monster 154

movies, not in reality." 158

"This is happening to you," the fish proclaimed. "I'm a goldfish, and I'm speaking 172

to you, young man. You've ignored me since the day you got me. For one thing, the 189

water in this bowl is too cold. Just dip your finger in it, and test it yourself. I don't 208

know how I've survived under these cruel conditions." 216

Of course, the water in the bowl wasn't too cold for the goldfish, but how was Tad 233

to know? How was Tad to know that his goldfish was not an ordinary fish, and as 250

soon as he dipped his finger into the water, he would trade places with the goldfish? 266

Tad stuck his finger in the water and found it was cold, but not freezing. "It feels 283

just fine to me," he tried to say, but no sound escaped him. Tad was now trapped in 301

the fish bowl, and the goldfish had become a little boy. Tad swam around the fish 317

bowl frantically, but when he tried to speak, only bubbles came out of his mouth. He 333

watched his fish, who was now a boy, move around his bedroom. 345

"I think I'll try to see one of those monster movies you mentioned," he told 360

Tad. "Goodbye, Tadpole." 363

SCORE _____ − _____ = _____
words attempted in one minute / number of errors / words correct per minute (wcpm)

The Writer's Club was an interesting group of talented school children who loved to write. Their faculty advisor suggested an interesting project for them. Each of them would write one paragraph of a story that would be printed in the school newspaper. The suggestion was eagerly accepted by participants. Joanie, the sports star of the school, began the story. She wrote this paragraph:

"Judy sat in class and watched her friend's gym class play soccer. She wished so hard that she could be excused from class and play with them. Suddenly, her teacher saw her looking outside and said, 'Why don't you go and play with them?' Judy didn't sit there another minute. She grabbed her books and folders and ran out to the field. She joined the soccer team and immediately scored a goal. She was awesome!"

Next was Scott's turn. He was a fan of science fiction.

"Just as Judy scored the winning soccer goal, aliens beamed her aboard their ship and flew off. Two large alien guards came at her to seize her and throw her into a cell. Judy gave the two of them a swift kick to the shins and seized control of their ship. She flew back to her school and waved at the students below."

It was Jessica's turn next. She loved movies, so she wrote about them.

"Then Judy flew off to California. She flew the spaceship right past the Hollywood sign and landed at a movie studio. One movie director asked if she would fly her spaceship for him in one of his movies. She said, 'Yes, but only if I can have the starring role.' The director agreed."

Finally it was Stephen's turn. The faculty advisor asked him to end the story with a nice conclusion.

"But Judy was bored as a movie star and with the spaceship, so she returned home and went to bed. The next day at school all her friends asked her what happened. All she said was, 'I scored the winning soccer goal.'"

The story was published in the school newspaper, and the readers requested a sequel.

The Writer's Club was an interesting group of talented school children who loved   13
to write. Their faculty advisor suggested an interesting project for them. Each of   26
them would write one paragraph of a story that would be printed in the school   41
newspaper. The suggestion was eagerly accepted by participants. Joanie, the   51
sports star of the school, began the story. She wrote this paragraph: 63

"Judy sat in class and watched her friend's gym class play soccer. She wished   77
so hard that she could be excused from class and play with them. Suddenly, her   92
teacher saw her looking outside and said, 'Why don't you go and play with them?'   107
Judy didn't sit there another minute. She grabbed her books and folders and ran out   122
to the field. She joined the soccer team and immediately scored a goal. She was   137
awesome!"   138

Next was Scott's turn. He was a fan of science fiction.   149

"Just as Judy scored the winning soccer goal, aliens beamed her aboard their   162
ship and flew off. Two large alien guards came at her to seize her and throw her into   180
a cell. Judy gave the two of them a swift kick to the shins and seized control of their   199
ship. She flew back to her school and waved at the students below."   212

It was Jessica's turn next. She loved movies, so she wrote about them.   225

"Then Judy flew off to California. She flew the spaceship right past the   238
Hollywood sign and landed at a movie studio. One movie director asked if she   252
would fly her spaceship for him in one of his movies. She said, 'Yes, but only if I can   271
have the starring role.' The director agreed."   278

Finally it was Stephen's turn. The faculty advisor asked him to end the story with   293
a nice conclusion.   296

"But Judy was bored as a movie star and with the spaceship, so she returned   311
home and went to bed. The next day at school all her friends asked her what   327
happened. All she said was, 'I scored the winning soccer goal.'"   338

The story was published in the school newspaper, and the readers requested a   351
sequel.   352

SCORE	_____	−	_____	=	_____
	words attempted in one minute		number of errors		words correct per minute (wcpm)

Thelma's new neighbor was mighty odd. She knew her neighbor was strange from the moment the moving van pulled into the driveway of the house across the street. She knew he was different just as soon as she saw him walk up to the front door of his new house.

Thelma wanted to walk across the street and introduce herself, but her new neighbor's costume made her stop and stare. The man wore shiny black boots that came to his knees and a black top hat. He had a mustache that curled up at the ends and a peculiar sparkle that lit his chocolate brown eyes. Thelma watched as he threw open his front door, took a moment to look inside, and then abruptly swung around and walked back to the moving truck parked in his driveway.

"Well, come on," he shouted. "Make yourselves at home!"

Then, to Thelma's complete surprise, a gang of clowns stepped out of the back of the truck. A troupe of monkeys and many more exotic animals followed the clowns. Thelma saw a pair of zebras, a bearded lion, and a very large tiger. She gasped when she saw a mama elephant and her tiny baby.

"How could the circus be moving in across the street?" Thelma asked herself. "What would she and the other neighbors do about the noise that would surely be caused by their new neighbor with all his animals?"

Thelma stayed at home and sat by the telephone, waiting for her neighbors to call and complain about the new neighbor. She sat for hours but no one called. She could hear loud music and the sound of wild animals coming from the house across the street. Still, no one knocked on her door to ask her if she was annoyed with the noise.

At one o'clock in the morning, the phone rang. The voice on the other end had an Irish accent.

"Hi. I'm you're new neighbor," said the voice. "I'm having a party. All your friends are already here. Would you like to join us?"

Thelma's new neighbor was mighty odd. She knew her neighbor was strange   12

from the moment the moving van pulled into the driveway of the house across the   27

street. She knew he was different just as soon as she saw him walk up to the front   45

door of his new house.   50

Thelma wanted to walk across the street and introduce herself, but her new   63

neighbor's costume made her stop and stare. The man wore shiny black boots that   77

came to his knees and a black top hat. He had a mustache that curled up at the   95

ends and a peculiar sparkle that lit his chocolate brown eyes. Thelma watched as   109

he threw open his front door, took a moment to look inside, and then abruptly swung   125

around and walked back to the moving truck parked in his driveway.   137

"Well, come on," he shouted. "Make yourselves at home!"   146

Then, to Thelma's complete surprise, a gang of clowns stepped out of the back of   161

the truck. A troupe of monkeys and many more exotic animals followed the clowns.   175

Thelma saw a pair of zebras, a bearded lion, and a very large tiger. She gasped   191

when she saw a mama elephant and her tiny baby.   201

"How could the circus be moving in across the street?" Thelma asked herself.   214

"What would she and the other neighbors do about the noise that would surely be   229

caused by their new neighbor with all his animals?"   238

Thelma stayed at home and sat by the telephone, waiting for her neighbors to   252

call and complain about the new neighbor. She sat for hours but no one called. She   268

could hear loud music and the sound of wild animals coming from the house across   283

the street. Still, no one knocked on her door to ask her if she was annoyed with the   301

noise.   302

At one o'clock in the morning, the phone rang. The voice on the other end had   318

an Irish accent.   321

"Hi. I'm you're new neighbor," said the voice. "I'm having a party. All your   335

friends are already here. Would you like to join us?"   345

SCORE	_____	−	_____	=	_____
	words attempted in one minute		number of errors		words correct per minute (wcpm)

Theodore was an actor in movies. He was not a big movie star, but he did like to act. He was called an extra. You see extras acting in movies all the time. Just look at all the people walking down a street in a movie scene. Those people are all extras. When you watch a movie and see people standing around in the background, you are watching the extras at work.

Theodore's last acting job was to play a police officer in a big Hollywood movie. Before beginning work, Theodore needed to put on some makeup. In the movies, women and girls aren't the only ones who wear makeup. A makeup artist helped put the makeup on Theodore's face. The makeup made him look good on film. Then Theodore had to put on a costume. His costume was a police officer's uniform. When he wore the costume, he looked just like a real police officer. Even though he wasn't really a police officer, he sure looked like one. He even had a gun in his holster. The gun wasn't real and it couldn't fire bullets, but it did look real enough for a movie.

Once Theodore was ready, he had to wait. He waited while the cameramen moved their cameras into place. He and the other actors waited for the director to tell them where to stand and what to do. The director told Theodore to jump out of the way when the star of the movie rode by him on a horse. He would have to be careful so the horse wouldn't run into him.

"Action!" yelled the director. The actors started performing. Theodore did everything the director told him to do. He acted like a police officer, and when the star rode by on the horse, Theodore jumped out of the way. Theodore was a good actor, but he wasn't really acting this time. He really did need to jump out of the way of the horse! Theodore and the other actors worked all night to make the scene just right. When the movie was finished, it was fun for Theodore's friends and family to see him on the big screen.

Theodore was an actor in movies. He was not a big movie star, but he did like to   18

act. He was called an extra. You see extras acting in movies all the time. Just look   35

at all the people walking down a street in a movie scene. Those people are all   51

extras. When you watch a movie and see people standing around in the   64

background, you are watching the extras at work.   72

Theodore's last acting job was to play a police officer in a big Hollywood movie.   87

Before beginning work, Theodore needed to put on some makeup. In the movies,   100

women and girls aren't the only ones who wear makeup. A makeup artist helped put   115

the makeup on Theodore's face. The makeup made him look good on film. Then   129

Theodore had to put on a costume. His costume was a police officer's uniform.   143

When he wore the costume, he looked just like a real police officer. Even though he   159

wasn't really a police officer, he sure looked like one. He even had a gun in his   176

holster. The gun wasn't real and it couldn't fire bullets, but it did look real enough for   193

a movie.   195

Once Theodore was ready, he had to wait. He waited while the cameramen   208

moved their cameras into place. He and the other actors waited for the director to   223

tell them where to stand and what to do. The director told Theodore to jump out of   240

the way when the star of the movie rode by him on a horse. He would have to be   259

careful so the horse wouldn't run into him.   267

"Action!" yelled the director. The actors started performing. Theodore did   277

everything the director told him to do. He acted like a police officer, and when the   293

star rode by on the horse, Theodore jumped out of the way. Theodore was a good   309

actor, but he wasn't really acting this time. He really did need to jump out of the way   327

of the horse! Theodore and the other actors worked all night to make the scene just   343

right. When the movie was finished, it was fun for Theodore's friends and family to   358

see him on the big screen.   364

SCORE	_____	−	_____	=	_____
	words attempted in one minute		number of errors		words correct per minute (wcpm)

There was a cave in the forest not far from Scarlett's house. Weeds and brambles half blocked the opening to the cave, but the local kids still knew where to find it. They gathered there on summer evenings before the sun set and dared each other to go inside. So far, no one had been daring enough to enter because they knew caves were dark and dangerous.

Scarlett, like the other children, was wary of the cave. But the cave also made her curious because she'd heard that bats often lived inside caves. She'd also heard that pirates sometimes hid their treasure in caves. "Maybe," she thought, "there is pirate treasure in the cave in the forest. Maybe if I am brave enough to go inside I'll find a treasure chest waiting for me filled with diamonds and rubies."

After many days, Scarlett talked her best friend, Millie, into helping her look for treasure in the cave. One evening they ventured into the cave with a set of lanterns.

"Don't be frightened, Millie," Scarlett whispered outside the cave. "Don't you want to be rich? There's pirate gold in there, Millie. I just know there is. We could both be wearing ruby earrings in school tomorrow."

Millie looked into the dark cave. Even though she was holding a lantern, she couldn't make out the depth of the cave. She'd tried to talk Scarlett out of this adventure, but she knew it was no use. When Scarlett had her mind set to do something, she did it.

Millie followed quietly behind Scarlett as she entered the cave. After walking about a hundred feet, Scarlett suddenly wobbled and pitched forward. Millie caught her around her waist just in time. The girls looked down and saw they were standing at the edge of a large hole. After that scare, they gave up and headed out of the cave. Once they were both safe and out in the open again, Millie sighed with relief.

"So much for pirate's treasure," Millie said.

"I do like this purple rock I found, but I don't think it was worth the trouble," Scarlett replied.

There was a cave in the forest not far from Scarlett's house. Weeds and   14

brambles half blocked the opening to the cave, but the local kids still knew where to   30

find it. They gathered there on summer evenings before the sun set and dared each   45

other to go inside. So far, no one had been daring enough to enter because they   61

knew caves were dark and dangerous.   67

Scarlett, like the other children, was wary of the cave. But the cave also made   82

her curious because she'd heard that bats often lived inside caves. She'd also   95

heard that pirates sometimes hid their treasure in caves. "Maybe," she thought,   107

"there is pirate treasure in the cave in the forest. Maybe if I am brave enough to go   125

inside I'll find a treasure chest waiting for me filled with diamonds and rubies."   139

After many days, Scarlett talked her best friend, Millie, into helping her look for   153

treasure in the cave. One evening they ventured into the cave with a set of lanterns.   169

"Don't be frightened, Millie," Scarlett whispered outside the cave. "Don't you   180

want to be rich? There's pirate gold in there, Millie. I just know there is. We could   197

both be wearing ruby earrings in school tomorrow."   205

Millie looked into the dark cave. Even though she was holding a lantern, she   219

couldn't make out the depth of the cave. She'd tried to talk Scarlett out of this   235

adventure, but she knew it was no use. When Scarlett had her mind set to do   251

something, she did it.   255

Millie followed quietly behind Scarlett as she entered the cave. After walking   267

about a hundred feet, Scarlett suddenly wobbled and pitched forward. Millie caught   279

her around her waist just in time. The girls looked down and saw they were standing   295

at the edge of a large hole. After that scare, they gave up and headed out of the   313

cave. Once they were both safe and out in the open again, Millie sighed with relief.   329

"So much for pirate's treasure," Millie said.   336

"I do like this purple rock I found, but I don't think it was worth the trouble,"   353

Scarlett replied.   355

SCORE	_____	−	_____	=	_____
	words attempted in one minute		number of errors		words correct per minute (wcpm)

Fifth grade was my favorite year of school. My classmates were intelligent and fun, and our teacher, Mrs. Norton, was the best teacher in the school. She made everything fun. She turned learning into an interesting activity.

For example, Mrs. Norton created something called the Link-Up Program. For every book a student read, he or she was given a paper link to add to the chain of links taped to the wall in the hallway. If our class read enough books to stretch the chain all the way around the school, she would reward us with a big party at the end of the year. To get us started at a good pace, she offered another reward. The boy and girl who read the most books by October first would get to go out for lunch with Mrs. Norton. Guess what? I read the most books, so Mrs. Norton took my friend, Kim, and me to Bigburger for lunch.

Another interesting reward Mrs. Norton used was called the Chocolate Factory. If a student did an outstanding job on his or her homework assignment, he or she would go to the Chocolate Factory. The Chocolate Factory was a wooden box in the shape of a little white house. When you opened the house by lifting the roof, you could see all of the chocolate and other candy that filled the house. A student could use one hand to grab as much candy as he or she could carry back to his or her desk. If any candy fell on the floor, it went back into the house. When I was rewarded with a trip to the Chocolate Factory, I thought about how I could get the most chocolate. I dipped my hand in like a scoop and filled it with candy. Then I carefully carried the candy back to my desk. I had enough candy to share with my friends.

Mrs. Norton was a very patient and kind teacher. She always made learning more fun and rewarding. I will never forget my fifth grade class and all the fun we had. Thank you, Mrs. Norton!

Fifth grade was my favorite year of school. My classmates were intelligent and | 13

fun, and our teacher, Mrs. Norton, was the best teacher in the school. She made | 28

everything fun. She turned learning into an interesting activity. | 37

For example, Mrs. Norton created something called the Link-Up Program. For | 49

every book a student read, he or she was given a paper link to add to the chain of | 68

links taped to the wall in the hallway. If our class read enough books to stretch the | 85

chain all the way around the school, she would reward us with a big party at the end | 103

of the year. To get us started at a good pace, she offered another reward. The boy | 120

and girl who read the most books by October first would get to go out for lunch with | 138

Mrs. Norton. Guess what? I read the most books, so Mrs. Norton took my friend, | 153

Kim, and me to Bigburger for lunch. | 160

Another interesting reward Mrs. Norton used was called the Chocolate Factory. | 171

If a student did an outstanding job on his or her homework assignment, he or she | 187

would go to the Chocolate Factory. The Chocolate Factory was a wooden box in the | 202

shape of a little white house. When you opened the house by lifting the roof, you | 218

could see all of the chocolate and other candy that filled the house. A student could | 234

use one hand to grab as much candy as he or she could carry back to his or her | 253

desk. If any candy fell on the floor, it went back into the house. When I was | 270

rewarded with a trip to the Chocolate Factory, I thought about how I could get the | 286

most chocolate. I dipped my hand in like a scoop and filled it with candy. Then I | 303

carefully carried the candy back to my desk. I had enough candy to share with my | 319

friends. | 320

Mrs. Norton was a very patient and kind teacher. She always made learning | 333

more fun and rewarding. I will never forget my fifth grade class and all the fun we | 350

had. Thank you, Mrs. Norton! | 355

SCORE	_____	−	_____	=	_____
	words attempted in one minute		number of errors		words correct per minute (wcpm)

Traveling is a lot of fun. Sometimes I travel so I can learn, and sometimes I travel just because I like to see different things. Sometimes I travel just to have fun and to keep from being bored. I have enjoyed traveling to ten different countries. Each country offered different and exciting things to see and do.

One of the most interesting countries I visited was Japan. Things are very different in Japan than they are in the United States of America. For example, the Japanese people speak Japanese, not English. They eat raw fish and rice instead of pizza. Some people wear robes instead of suits. The people in Japan are very kind and thoughtful, but it is hard to understand their customs.

France is another country that was fun to visit. The capital of France is Paris. Paris is a beautiful city with many interesting things to see. I saw the Eiffel Tower, one of the most famous buildings in the world. One of the biggest museums in the world is also in Paris. It is home to some of the most famous paintings in the world. The food is very good in France. They make good cheese and pastries. If you ever have a chance, you should go to France.

Ukraine is another country which is very different from America. The people in Ukraine do not all have cars or new clothes, and their food is a little different from our food. But the people are very loving and fun to know. They are very kind to visitors from the United States. If you go to Ukraine, try as much of the good food as you can.

Mexico is also a fun country to visit. In Mexico City, you can speak Spanish and eat burritos. In the coastal areas, you can swim in the ocean. There are many things to buy in Mexico, like blankets, pottery, and clothing. Many people from the Unites States visit Mexico because the two countries are so close together.

If you ever have a chance to travel, do not pass up the opportunity. You can have great adventures in other places.

Traveling is a lot of fun. Sometimes I travel so I can learn, and sometimes I   16

travel just because I like to see different things. Sometimes I travel just to have fun   32

and to keep from being bored. I have enjoyed traveling to ten different countries.   46

Each country offered different and exciting things to see and do.   57

One of the most interesting countries I visited was Japan. Things are very   70

different in Japan than they are in the United States of America. For example, the   85

Japanese people speak Japanese, not English. They eat raw fish and rice instead   98

of pizza. Some people wear robes instead of suits. The people in Japan are very   113

kind and thoughtful, but it is hard to understand their customs.   124

France is another country that was fun to visit. The capital of France is Paris.   139

Paris is a beautiful city with many interesting things to see. I saw the Eiffel Tower,   155

one of the most famous buildings in the world. One of the biggest museums in the   171

world is also in Paris. It is home to some of the most famous paintings in the world.   189

The food is very good in France. They make good cheese and pastries. If you ever   205

have a chance, you should go to France.   213

Ukraine is another country which is very different from America. The people in   226

Ukraine do not all have cars or new clothes, and their food is a little different from   243

our food. But the people are very loving and fun to know. They are very kind to   260

visitors from the United States. If you go to Ukraine, try as much of the good food as   278

you can.   280

Mexico is also a fun country to visit. In Mexico City, you can speak Spanish and   296

eat burritos. In the coastal areas, you can swim in the ocean. There are many   311

things to buy in Mexico, like blankets, pottery, and clothing. Many people from the   325

Unites States visit Mexico because the two countries are so close together.   337

If you ever have a chance to travel, do not pass up the opportunity. You can   353

have great adventures in other places.   359

SCORE	_____	−	_____	=	_____
	words attempted in one minute		number of errors		words correct per minute (wcpm)

When Maggie Ray's mother told her they would visit Mrs. Zale at teatime next Thursday, Maggie Ray said she wasn't going. Mrs. Zale lived in the big house on the corner of the block. Mrs. Zale's yard was filled with dead trees and surrounded by a tall, spiked fence. The curtains over Mrs. Zale's windows were never pulled open, and her house was always dark at night. Mrs. Zale didn't seem to have any visitors except the mailman when he delivered her mail.

On Wednesday, Maggie Ray cornered the mailman. "What's Mrs. Zale like? I'm supposed to go to her house on Thursday for tea, and I need to know."

The mailman smiled at Maggie Ray. "Don't tell me you've never met Mrs. Zale. You've lived down the street from her for over a year."

"Well I haven't," Maggie Ray said. "But I have to meet her tomorrow. Do you think you could tell me a bit about her?"

"Oh, no," the mailman said. "Mrs. Zale will want you to be surprised."

When teatime rolled around the next day, Maggie Ray's mother had to drag Maggie Ray up the sidewalk to Mrs. Zale's front door.

"I don't want to go in there," Maggie Ray panted. "Please don't make me go in there."

Before Maggie Ray could escape from her mother's grip, the front door opened. Maggie Ray's eyes nearly fell out of her head when a monkey in a red velvet vest opened the door. The monkey squawked at Maggie Ray and her mother and pointed them toward the dining room.

The dining room held another surprise. A parrot was sitting on the chandelier.

"Hello, hello, hello," he said as they walked into the room. "Would you like cream or sugar, cream or sugar?"

Maggie Ray couldn't believe her eyes. A silver tea service was laid out on the dining room table. There were trays of cookies, tarts, candies, and chocolates.

"Welcome, welcome," said the old woman who stepped into the room. She was dressed in an emerald ball gown. "I'm so glad you could make it, Maggie Ray." Mrs. Zale really was full of surprises!

Name _____   Date _____

When Maggie Ray's mother told her they would visit Mrs. Zale at teatime next   14

Thursday, Maggie Ray said she wasn't going. Mrs. Zale lived in the big house on   29

the corner of the block. Mrs. Zale's yard was filled with dead trees and surrounded   44

by a tall, spiked fence. The curtains over Mrs. Zale's windows were never pulled   58

open, and her house was always dark at night. Mrs. Zale didn't seem to have any   74

visitors except the mailman when he delivered her mail.   83

On Wednesday, Maggie Ray cornered the mailman. "What's Mrs. Zale like? I'm   95

supposed to go to her house on Thursday for tea, and I need to know."   110

The mailman smiled at Maggie Ray. "Don't tell me you've never met Mrs. Zale.   124

You've lived down the street from her for over a year."   135

"Well I haven't," Maggie Ray said. "But I have to meet her tomorrow. Do you   150

think you could tell me a bit about her?"   159

"Oh, no," the mailman said. "Mrs. Zale will want you to be surprised."   172

When teatime rolled around the next day, Maggie Ray's mother had to drag   185

Maggie Ray up the sidewalk to Mrs. Zale's front door.   195

"I don't want to go in there," Maggie Ray panted. "Please don't make me go in   211

there."   212

Before Maggie Ray could escape from her mother's grip, the front door opened.   225

Maggie Ray's eyes nearly fell out of her head when a monkey in a red velvet vest   242

opened the door. The monkey squawked at Maggie Ray and her mother and   255

pointed them toward the dining room.   261

The dining room held another surprise. A parrot was sitting on the chandelier.   274

"Hello, hello, hello," he said as they walked into the room. "Would you like cream   289

or sugar, cream or sugar?"   294

Maggie Ray couldn't believe her eyes. A silver tea service was laid out on the   309

dining room table. There were trays of cookies, tarts, candies, and chocolates.   321

"Welcome, welcome," said the old woman who stepped into the room. She was   334

dressed in an emerald ball gown. "I'm so glad you could make it, Maggie Ray." Mrs.   350

Zale really was full of surprises!   356

SCORE	_____	−	_____	=	_____
	words attempted in one minute		number of errors		words correct per minute (wcpm)

Name _____

Progress Monitoring Report

DIRECTIONS Draw a goal line for the student in pencil, based on the expected Rate of Improvement (ROI) for the student's grade-level reading ability. Mark a dot for words read correctly per minute (wcpm) on each weekly assessment. Compare to the goal in order to determine whether instruction needs to be adjusted or whether a more challenging goal needs to be set. (Mark a vertical line to show the date of any instructional intervention so that you can see its effect.) Connect the dots to show progress over the year.

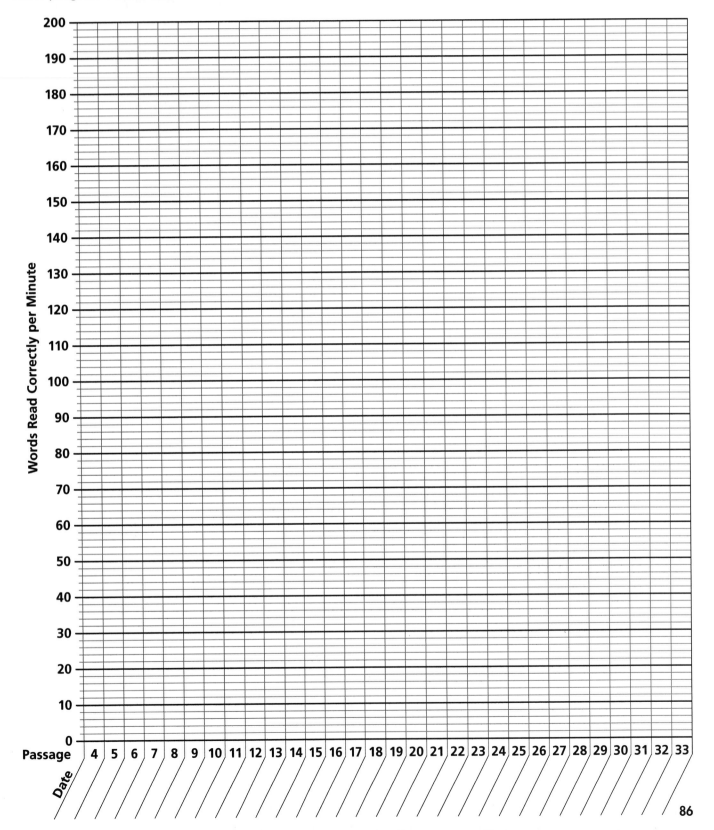